Living Bread

Living Bread

David Goode

CANTERBURY
PRESS
Norwich

© David Goode 2006

First published in 2006
by the Canterbury Press Norwich
(a publishing imprint of Hymns Ancient & Modern Limited,
a registered charity)
9–17 St Alban's Place
London N1 0NX

www.scm-canterburypress.co.uk

British Library Cataloguing in Publication data

A catalogue record for this book is available
from the British Library

ISBN 1-85311-687-4
978-1-85311-687-2

Typeset by Regent Typesetting, London
Printed and bound by
Bookmarque, Croydon, Surrey

For Sam

Contents

Acknowledgements   xi
Foreword   xiii
Abstract   xv
Preface   xvii

Introduction   1

  Do this in remembrance of me   2
  The wedding banquet   6
  Preparing for communion   10
    Careful preparation   12
    Repentance: examine yourselves   14
    Discernment: recognizing the body   17
    Thanksgiving: true eucharist   20

1 **Repentance**   23

  A selection of prayers of repentance   24
  Bishop Brian Duppa's Guide for the Penitent   27
    A litany of confession   28
    The penitent's prayer   35

2 **Discernment**   38

3 **Thanksgiving**   49

4 **Taylor's Holy Living**   58

Meditation on the Passion   58
Prayers of intercession   63
  For ourselves   63
  For the whole Catholic Church   64
  For all Christian rulers and governors   64
  For all that minister about holy things   65
  For our nearest relatives   65
  For our parents, friends and benefactors   66
  For all in difficulty   66
  For all pregnant women and for unborn children   67
  For all men and women in the Christian Church   67
Preparation for the Holy Sacrament   70
  An act of love   70
  An act of desire   70
  An act of contrition   71
  An act of faith   71
A prayer before receiving   72
After receiving the consecrated and blessed bread   72
After receiving the cup of blessing   73

Conclusion   75

Appendix 1: Brief biographies   78

  Archbishop William Laud   78
  Bishop Lancelot Andrewes   80
  Bishop Brian Duppa   81
  Bishop Thomas Ken   82
  Bishop Simon Patrick   84
  Bishop Jeremy Taylor   85
  Bishop Thomas Wilson   87
  Leo the Great   89
  Gregory the Great   89

John Chrysostom   90
Augustine of Hippo   91

Appendix 2: Pre-Reformation prayers   94

The Western Churches   94
  Preparation prayers   94
  Thanksgiving prayers   97
The Eastern Churches   98
  Preparation prayers   98
  Thanksgiving prayers   100

Appendix 3: Scriptural imagery in prayer   102

Appendix 4: Texts used for this book   105

Laud's *Private Devotions*   105
Andrewes' *Private Devotions*   106
Duppa's *Guide for the Penitent*   106
Duppa's *Holy Rules and Helps*   106
Ken's *Manual of Prayers*   107
Patrick's *Book for Beginners*   107
Taylor's *Holy Living*   107
Wilson's *Lord's Supper*   108
Anonymous *Guide to Young Communicants*   108

Acknowledgements

The author is indebted to many people for this book.

To the University Librarian and staff of the Rare Books Room at the University Library in Cambridge, particularly to Nicholas Smith.

To Dr Petà Dunstan, Librarian of the Faculty of Divinity.

To Chadwyck-Healey for their excellent service *Early English Books Online* (EEBO), which has saved the author nothing short of a fortune in time and travel.

To the owners of the many second-hand and antiquarian bookshops who have cheerfully relieved the author of most of that fortune.

To the author's father, Canon Peter Goode, who loves the Caroline Divines; and to the author's mother, Margaret, who is entirely ambivalent towards the Caroline Divines but loves the author.

To the author's wife, Sam, for risking plague and pestilence every time he brought yet another diseased and mite-ridden old book home.

To Dr Augustine Casiday of Durham for his help with translating some of Archbishop Laud's rather difficult Latin.

To the Reverend Doctor John Jillions, Dean of Annunciation-St Nicholas Orthodox Cathedral in Ottawa, for his friendship and support and cheeky jibes about liturgical archaeologists.

To my friends and colleagues in the Faculty of Divinity.

To all the others who at sundry times and in divers manners

have helped but who cannot be acknowledged in person, either through multiplicity of names or the author's forgetfulness.

Thank you.

Foreword

Celebrating the eucharist is the joy as well as the duty of all who follow Jesus Christ: 'Do this in remembrance of me'. More frequent celebrations of the sacrament, as well as encouragement of the faithful to receive more often, became the pattern through the twentieth century and indicated a deepening of eucharistic understanding. Ironically, however, the greater familiarity took away some of the awe and reverence in which the sacrament was held. In the twenty-first century, many Christians have come almost to take it for granted.

It can come as a shock therefore to delve into this new and welcome book and find the seriousness with which our forebears took the reception of the eucharist. There is no last-minute slipping into church to participate but instead a thorough and thoughtful preparation for the most holy of feasts. Key to it is a sense of unworthiness to meet God so intimately without first having examined one's conscience and expressed sorrow for one's mistakes, and given thanks for all the gifts we so undeservedly receive.

In today's world, repentance is unfashionable, as psychological insights have made us wary of guilt and its neurotic associations. But truly to repent is to renew and cleanse the spirit, and the great Christian divines, from whose writings the prayers here are gathered, understood the importance of this process. It clears the heart and mind and soul so as to be at our most open to God in the sacrament. The more open we are, the more we can act as channels for God's transforming grace in the world.

The eucharist is a Christian's comfort but also it is his or her greatest challenge: a challenge to live the Christian life in its fullness. For that, we need to prepare, and the treasures in this book help us to do just that.

Petà Dunstan
Advent 2005

Abstract

In the past, Christians took preparation for receiving the holy communion seriously. In recent years, this preparation has, to a large extent, fallen by the wayside. But there is renewed interest: *Common Worship* begins the general notes to the service of Holy Communion by saying: 'Careful devotional preparation before the service is recommended for every communicant' and gives one form of preparation.

In the Church of England, the finest forms of preparation were produced by bishops of the seventeenth century in guides for communicants, and printed in large numbers. The depth of these guides to receiving the holy communion is unmatched in any other form of preparation, from any other church, before or since.

Despite the exquisite beauty of these prayers, their style of language means they are torturous to use today in their original form, and they have become almost completely forgotten: sparkling gems hidden under the accumulation of linguistic and grammatical change over the last four hundred years.

Now, the very best of these forms of preparation have been researched and collected into one volume. Careful editing into contemporary language means the original beauty and depth of thought is retained, but they are now available in clear and easy-to-understand English: timeless wisdom for the twenty-first-century communicant.

From the pens, and hearts, of some of the Church of

England's finest theologians, such as Archbishop William Laud, Bishops Lancelot Andrewes, Brian Duppa, Thomas Ken, Simon Patrick, Jeremy Taylor, Thomas Wilson, and others who left their work but not their names, a large selection of litanies, prayers, meditations and thanksgivings is once again available to help with the careful devotional preparation required for a worthy reception of the holy communion.

Preface

Repentance is the 'key to the kingdom'. Sincere recognition of our failings, apology if they involve and drag down others, amendment of life: all of these are necessary steps, not just to a worthy reception of the holy communion, but to a worthy life.

This book will help the reader both to understand and to put into practice the importance of preparing carefully for the holy communion, and the book, like the preparation, begins with repentance, and only then moves on to discernment and thanksgiving.

But it is important to keep repentance in proportion. A sickly or mournful beating up of the self is no good. It is especially useless if it leads to a short period of overly pious self-pity followed by the rest of the day, or the week, or the month, spent without any remembrance of either the sins or the forgiving nature of God's mercy.

And the surest antidote to this is simple: practice. Repentance must not become a perfunctory listing of faults, or a mournful burst of self-pity, or a pessimistic shrugging of shoulders at our incurable sinfulness.

The prayers in this collection have been carefully chosen to give a good balance between repentance, discernment, and thanksgiving. But there is no getting away from the fact that repentance is first: the others follow.

Choose one or more prayers from each section, but do not overdo it. These are not three services to be said from start to finish, but three collections to be used as the basis for each of the three stages of preparation.

There is a complete system in this book, devised by Bishop Jeremy Taylor. But this is something the reader should work towards, not launch into, and (apart from the prayers of intercession, which really do need to be taken as a whole) should be used as something for the reader to take prayers from rather than read as a whole except on the odd occasion.

Probably the most effective way to use the prayers in this collection is to use them as part of a rule of life. The idea of a rule of life is not new and is too big a subject to treat lightly here, and needs guidance to be really effective. A rule of life should, though, include a rule of prayer. A rule of daily prayer. And this rule of prayer should include self-examination and space for repentance.

When we are able to live, to the best of individual abilities, a rule of life that weaves prayer with repentance every single day, then we are practising true repentance. And true repentance, as we know, is always received and accepted by God.

True penitence, therefore, is a life-long thing; a perennial flow of godly sorrow, not the gushing of a fountain once opened to be quickly closed; an abiding state, not a passing paroxysm; a clothing which the saint lays not aside until it be exchanged for the robe made white in the blood of the Lamb . . .

Recall therefore the hated past, not to diminish hope, but to increase godly sorrow; not to cloud the vision of the Redeemer, but to deepen the sense of his loving forgiveness; not to lessen the recovered power, but to infuse into this power a profounder tenderness; not to separate from God, but to unite with him by a firmer and a closer bond.

Review the past, that a deeper penitence may awake in the present. Deepen the penitence, that a tenderer spirit may enter into the life; that a deepening tenderness may receive a greater grace. Seek to be found at last in the humility of the returning prodigal, who, having cast all away to win heaven, returns in his homeward track with the one end absorbing all other thoughts and aims, and yet preserves the thought that the hired servant's place in his own father's home is all he merits and can claim.

Look well and see, not merely if there be any way of wickedness in you, but what your repentance has been, its motives, its depths, its reality, the truth of its sorrow, the honesty of its purpose, the fullness of its resolves, the perseverance of its resistance of sin, its progress from grace to grace, and 'from glory to glory, even as by the Spirit of the Lord'.

How many have failed, because too soon they left off their penitential garb, and ceased to utter their penitential acts! How many stunted growths even of true life have there been, in consequence of imperfect repentances! How many, all their life long, are beset with old sins, and lingering returns of early life, because their foundations were not laid low, nor grounded on an acceptable penance!

Test your very repentance, that it be a repentance not to be repented of. Bear in mind that the very terror of the judgement consists in the startling truth, that it must fall first on the heirs of the kingdom:

'For the time is come that judgement must begin at the house of God; and if it first begin at us, what shall the end be of them that obey not the gospel of God? And if the righteous scarcely be saved, where shall the ungodly and the sinner appear?'

'Penitence lifelong', the first of a series of six lectures entitled

'The life of penitence' delivered at All Saints, Margaret Street, by Reverend T. T. Carter during Lent 1866.

David Goode
Faculty of Divinity, Cambridge
Advent 2005

Introduction

Since the very earliest days, Christians have met together, at least on the Lord's Day, to break the bread and to give thanks, as the Acts of the Apostles and the history of the very early Church testify. This taking of bread, and giving thanks over it, is both the basis for the service of the Eucharist, and also the origin of its name: Paul, when recounting the events to the Church at Corinth, says that Christ took the bread and then '*ευχαριστησας*', when he had 'given thanks', gave it to his disciples.

These words are something we hear every Sunday, at least. But how often do we stop to think of the wonder of this act? The writer to the Hebrews, as he was writing to converts from Judaism to Christianity, makes a great deal of comparing the Christ with the Old Testament. He draws out example after example of how the Christ fulfils in every respect the scriptures. One particularly poignant comparison is how the Christ became:

> *a merciful and faithful high priest in the service of God, to make a sacrifice of atonement for the sins of the people.*
>
> Hebrews 2.17

Under the old covenant, the high priests shed blood, poured it out, for the sins of the people. In this, the early Church Fathers saw a type, a figure, of the Christ. But there is a crucial difference between the high priests of the old covenant and the merciful faithful high priest who is the Christ: while the high priests poured out the blood of a dumb animal, the Christ poured out his own blood for our salvation. Christ is both priest and victim in this mysterious sacrifice:

> *At the last great supper lying,*
> *circled by his brethren band,*
> *meekly with the law complying,*
> *first he finished its command;*
> *then, Immortal Food supplying,*
> *gave himself with his own hand*

The hymn 'Pange lingua gloriosi', St Thomas Aquinas

What a mysterious and strange thing: the Christ, the Priest-Victim, went to his voluntary suffering and death for us after he had solemnly shown his inner circle of friends what was about to happen by giving them himself with his own hand.

Do this in remembrance of me

The Eucharist is, in part, a memorial or remembrance of that great night, something we do in fulfilment of Christ's command that we continue to 'do this in remembrance of me' (Luke 22.19). 'Do this', he says: not a polite request, or a friendly suggestion, but an order; not an option, but a mandate.

It is a looking back, in a very similar way to the Jewish Passover of today, where the old story of the chosen people's escape from the hands of the oppressor is told again each year, by the old to the young, so as the young are taught never to forget God's great blessing on his chosen people, and the covenant he made with them, that he will be their God and they shall be his people.

The supper on that great night was, as the Gospels tell us, a Passover supper. Just before Paul tells the Corinthians that they proclaim the Lord's death until his glorious return, he reminds them that their ancestors, too, had been shown a fore-taste of Christ:

> I do not want you to be unaware, brothers and sisters, that our ancestors were all under the cloud, and all passed through the sea, and all were baptized into Moses in the cloud and in the sea, and all ate the same spiritual food, and all drank the same spiritual drink. For they drank from the spiritual rock that followed them, and the rock was Christ.
>
> 1 Corinthians 10.1–4

And now the one who had given the law to Moses, the law that was 'our disciplinarian until Christ came' (Galatians 3.24), was himself meekly complying with that law.

Christ's compliance with that law was twofold. He was, as a pious Jew, complying in the sense that he was fulfilling God's order to Moses that the people should never forget that other great night that this great night was remembering: the deliver-ance of the chosen people from the hand of Pharaoh. God had told Moses:

> Remember this day on which you came out of Egypt, out of the house of slavery . . . You shall keep this ordinance at its proper time from year to year.
>
> Exodus 13.3a, 10

But, as the Christ and his friends were eating the Pass-over meal, something new and shocking was in store for the disciples. Having complied with the letter of the law in eating the Passover meal, the Christ

> took a loaf of bread, and when he had given thanks, he

*broke it and said, 'This is my body that is for you. Do this
in remembrance of me.' In the same way he took the cup
also, after supper, saying, 'This cup is the new covenant in
my blood. Do this, as often as you drink it, in remembrance
of me.'*

1 Corinthians 11.23b–25

He took bread, blessed it, and returned it to them not as
mere bread, but as his body. He took the cup of wine that
was a traditional part of the Jewish Passover ritual, blessed
that, and returned it to his friends as the new covenant in his
blood.

The old covenant that God had made with Moses, and the
covenant the disciples had supposed they had come to remember in this great night, was complete, and a new covenant was
in place. All the prophecies written over thousands of years in
the scriptures were fulfilled in the Christ.

This all sounds very cosy and heart-warming, but we must
not for a moment lose sight of what the writer to the Hebrews
reminds his readers: that *not even the first covenant was
inaugurated without blood.*

*For when every commandment had been told to all the
people by Moses in accordance with the law, he took the
blood of calves and goats, with water and scarlet wool
and hyssop, and sprinkled both the scroll itself and all the
people, saying, 'This is the blood of the covenant that God
has ordained for you.'*

Hebrews 9.18–20

Just as the first covenant was not inaugurated without blood,
so the new covenant requires blood. Not, this time, the blood
of calves and goats, which for Moses was the blood of the old
covenant, but Christ's new covenant in his own blood.

The writer to the Hebrews also reminds his readers that 'under the law almost everything is purified with blood, and without the shedding of blood there is no forgiveness of sins' (Hebrews 9.22), and Christ tells his disciples that this is 'my blood of the covenant, which is poured out for many for the forgiveness of sins' (Matthew 26.28).

So, that Passover meal on that great night began as a compliance with the law, with the law-giver himself meekly complying with his own law, in order to fulfil it and to bring in the new covenant in his blood.

A simple act of remembering events long ago, a looking back, became, in an instant, a very real and shocking present for the disciples. They were not just remembering something, they were witnessing a new reality, the institution of a new covenant, like the old in some ways, but utterly new.

But the blood is not all we remember. Christ's voluntary passion and death was part of his saving work, but it is not right to concentrate solely on the doom, the suffering, the sacrifice. Our salvation required his death, but it also required his incarnation, his resurrection, his ascension, and his taking his seat at God's right hand in heaven.

The Church, as it developed the various seasons, has devoted the end of Lent, and particularly the end of Holy Week, to contemplating the passion and death of Christ. And, in a way, we remember that again every Sunday at least, and often daily. But the remembrance is in its place, along with the other great and mysterious events in our salvation.

The celebration of the eucharist is not a doom-laden and maudlin brooding on death and sacrifice. We do not worship a dead, blood-soaked, and lifeless God: we worship the living God, who died and rose again for us, so that we may 'have life, and have it abundantly' (John 10.10).

And, as the supper that great night came to its climactic end, Christ gave them not mere bread, but his own body, not mere wine, but his own blood. He supplied them not with bread 'like that which your ancestors ate', and which they thought they had come to remember, but with 'the bread that came down from heaven'.

Even though their ancestors ate bread, Christ told them some time before, 'they died. But the one who eats this bread will live for ever' (John 6.58). But now, we can eat not just 'bread to strengthen the human heart' and 'wine to gladden the human heart' (Psalm 104.15b, 14b), but the 'living bread' (John 6.51).

The wedding banquet

Down the years, one of the most popular likenesses of the Eucharist has been the banquet or feast:

> *Jesus spoke to them in parables, saying: 'The kingdom of heaven may be compared to a king who gave a wedding banquet for his son. He sent his slaves to call those who had been invited to the wedding banquet, but they would not come. Again he sent other slaves, saying, "Tell those who have been invited: Look, I have prepared my dinner, my oxen and my fat calves have been slaughtered, and everything is ready; come to the wedding banquet." But they made light of it and went away, one to his farm, another to his business, while the rest seized his slaves, maltreated them, and killed them. The king was enraged. He sent his troops, destroyed those murderers, and burned their city. Then he said to his slaves, "The wedding is ready, but those invited were not worthy. Go therefore into the main streets, and invite everyone you find to the wedding banquet." Those slaves went out into the streets and gathered all whom they*

found, both good and bad; so the wedding hall was filled with guests.

Matthew 22.1–10

There is not space in this introduction to pick apart all the levels of meaning in this parable. But there is space to say a little about it. The most obvious is that this is an allegory of God the Father, God the Son, and that we, the Gentiles, are those invited the second time.

That great pastor, St Gregory the Great, preached a sermon on this Gospel reading (*Forty Gospel Homilies*, number 38). After dealing with some differences between this and a similar parable related in Luke's Gospel, Gregory goes on to give a superb explanation.

The king is our Father in heaven, who has prepared a banquet to celebrate the mystical marriage of his Son to the spouse, the Church, through the mystery of his incarnation. The womb of the Virgin was his bridal chamber, and at his incarnation in flesh, he 'comes out like a bridegroom from his wedding canopy' (Psalm 19.5), and now his Father wants to celebrate the marriage with a feast.

But those who were first invited do not come. They make excuses. One goes to his farm, which Gregory sees as representing those who care more for toiling on this earth than for toiling for the heavenly kingdom. Another goes off to his business, which Gregory sees as representing those who are more interested in storing up treasures on earth than treasures in heaven (Matthew 6.19–21). Neither sort gives any thought to the mystery of the incarnation.

The slaves the king had sent to announce the good news of the marriage banquet, and to issue the invitations, are killed by the very people invited to the feast. In another place, Christ laments over Jerusalem, saying 'Jerusalem, Jerusalem, the city that kills the prophets and stones those who are sent to it!'

(Luke 13.34), showing the ingratitude of those first invited, and the fate of many who were sent: the lucky ones were ignored, the unlucky ones killed, but either way, those invited rejected the invitation.

So, the invitation is extended. The king invites people who would previously have been considered unworthy, and Gregory interprets the main streets as our actions, and the streets (often translated 'byways') means our failed actions. He notes that it is often those who are not prosperous in this life, the downcast, who come readily to God.

The wedding banquet is now filled. Almost indiscriminately, the good and the bad together, the banquet goes ahead. Gregory interprets this mixture of good and bad in one feast as the Church today, which contains all sorts. Though the Church brings all to faith, it does not always lead all of its members to the freedom of spiritual grace because some will continue to obscure their true state with sins.

Now this would be a lovely, warm, fuzzy story if this were the end of it. But Christ often told parables that sound all lovely but have a sting in the tail. The parable continues:

'But when the king came in to see the guests, he noticed a man there who was not wearing a wedding robe, and he said to him, "Friend, how did you get in here without a wedding robe?" And he was speechless. Then the king said to the attendants, "Bind him hand and foot, and throw him into the outer darkness, where there will be weeping and gnashing of teeth." For many are called, but few are chosen.'

Matthew 22.11–14

We must be aware, says Gregory, alert against the very real possibility that having been invited to the feast, the king should come and find fault with some aspect of our wedding robe, the robe that clothes the heart.

What, Gregory asks, is meant by the wedding robe? Well, it is not baptism, for all who are in the Church were baptized. Is it faith? No. Most people have faith, or at least hope. What else, Gregory asks, could it be but love?

About 250 years before Gregory preached this sermon, another of the great Fathers of the Church, Augustine of Hippo, preached a similar sermon on the same passage, to his congregation under the hot North African sun.

Quoting the Apostle Paul's wise words to his spiritual son Timothy, Augustine also knows that love is the wedding robe, telling his hearers that 'the aim of such instruction is love that comes from a pure heart, a good conscience, and sincere faith' (1 Timothy 1.5).

This, says Augustine, is the wedding robe. Not any old love, as Christ points out, 'for if you love those who love you, what reward do you have? Do not even the tax-collectors do the same?' (Matthew 5.46).

No, it must be divine love, centred on Christ. It must be the love of Christ, that itself comes from the Father's love, both for his Son, and for us. As the Apostle Paul knows well, even

if I speak in the tongues of mortals and of angels, but do not have love, I am a noisy gong or a clanging cymbal. And if I have prophetic powers, and understand all mysteries and all knowledge, and if I have all faith, so as to remove mountains, but do not have love, I am nothing. If I give away all my possessions, and if I hand over my body so that I may boast, but do not have love, I gain nothing.

(1 Corinthians 13.1–3)

The scriptures teach us that faith is good. They teach us that hope is good. They teach us that love is good. 'And now faith, hope, and love abide, these three; and the greatest of these is love' (1 Corinthians 13.13).

Gregory and Augustine were both spot on: it has to be love. The King has showed his love by issuing invitations to his beloved Son's wedding banquet. He has showed his love by sending his Son to claim his Bride, the Church. He has showed his love by giving that Son over to torture and death, and by glorifying him by raising him from the dead, to establish a new covenant with all, and to make it so that his 'house shall be called a house of prayer for all peoples' (Isaiah 56.7). He has showed his love in that his Son gave himself once for all, but also in that we can feast with him and on him again and again, not only in his command to 'do this in remembrance of me' (1 Corinthians 11.24), but also in fulfilment of this promise to 'remember, I am with you always, to the end of the age' (Matthew 28.20).

'God is love, and those who abide in love abide in God, and God abides in them' (1 John 4.16b).

Preparing for communion

Whoever, therefore, eats the bread or drinks the cup of the Lord in an unworthy manner will be answerable for the body and blood of the Lord. Examine yourselves, and only then eat of the bread and drink of the cup. For all who eat and drink without discerning the body, eat and drink judgement against themselves. For this reason many of you are weak and ill, and some have died. But if we judged ourselves, we would not be judged. But when we are judged by the Lord, we are disciplined so that we may not be condemned along with the world.

(1 Corinthians 11.27–32)

Harsh words, indeed. Those who eat and drink without discerning the body become weak and ill? Some even die? If this was the fate of the Corinthians, barely a generation after Christ lived on earth with us, when his body was still a living memory of wonderful events only just past, what hope is there for us?

In delivering this stinging indictment of our approach to the holy communion, Paul also gives us the way to proceed, the key to proper preparation: examination first, then reception. From the earliest times, Christians have prepared themselves for receiving the communion by doing just that. And this almost always takes the same form: examination with repentance, discernment by recognition of what we are going to receive, and thanksgiving afterwards. This short introduction is divided into these three sections, as is the main book.

After some general comments on careful preparation, each section of this introduction looks at the three stages of preparation through the eyes of the early Church Fathers.

The first three sections of the book give practical advice, centred on prayer, from the works of the Church of England bishops of the seventeenth century, the so-called Caroline Divines who spanned the reigns of Charles I and Charles II with the difficult period between when Puritan powers looked for nothing less than the destruction of the Church of England, and from other less-well-known bishops around the same time.

Part Four gives a modern-English version of a complete system of preparation by Bishop Jeremy Taylor, first printed in his famous book *Holy Living*.

And finally the appendices: the first gives brief biographical details of the bishops; the second is a selection of prayers and thanksgivings from the pre-Reformation Church, the third a brief introduction to the scriptural imagery used in these prayers, and the fourth very brief descriptions of the primary sources used in the main part of this book.

All of these prayers collected here have been carefully re-searched and edited. Sometimes the editing has been light, but often rather more drastic. The author wonders if it might be more accurate to describe these prayers as 'based on' rather than 'from' the Caroline Divines as changes have been inevit-able, and a look at the originals will show that some liberty has been taken. But the author has tried to retain the intentions, and a little of the majesty, of the original prayers, and any failure to do them justice is entirely his.

Careful preparation

Though more often than not ignored these days, the Church of England spells out exactly what constitutes a proper prepara-tion in words that are, in their way, even more stark than St Paul's:

It is our duty to render most humble and hearty thanks to Almighty God our heavenly Father, for that he hath given his Son our Saviour Jesus Christ, not only to die for us, but also to be our spiritual food and sustenance in that holy Sacrament. Which being so divine and comfortable a thing to them who receive it worthily, and so dangerous to them that will presume to receive it unworthily; my duty is to exhort you in the mean season to consider the dignity of that holy mystery, and the great peril of the unworthy receiving thereof; and so to search and examine your own consciences, (and that not lightly, and after the manner of dissemblers with God; but so) that ye may come holy and clean to such a heavenly Feast, in the marriage-garment required by God in holy Scripture, and be received as worthy partakers of that holy Table.

The way and means thereto is; First, to examine your lives and conversations by the rule of God's commandments; and whereinsoever ye shall perceive yourselves to have offended, either by will, word, or deed, there to bewail your own sinfulness, and to confess yourselves to Almighty God, with full purpose of amendment of life.

And if ye shall perceive your offences to be such as are not only against God, but also against your neighbours; then ye shall reconcile yourselves unto them; being ready to make restitution and satisfaction, according to the uttermost of your powers, for all injuries and wrongs done by you to any other; and being likewise ready to forgive others that have offended you, as ye would have forgiveness of your offences at God's hand: for otherwise the receiving of the holy Communion doth nothing else but increase your damnation.

Therefore if any of you be a blasphemer of God, an hinderer or slanderer of his Word, an adulterer, or be in malice, or envy, or in any other grievous crime, repent you of your sins, or else come not to that holy Table; lest, after the taking of that holy Sacrament, the devil enter into you, as he entered into Judas, and fill you full of all iniquities, and bring you to destruction both of body and soul.

And because it is requisite, that no man should come to the holy Communion, but with a full trust in God's mercy, and with a quiet conscience; therefore if there be any of you, who by this means cannot quiet his own conscience herein, but requireth further comfort or counsel, let him come to me, or to some other discreet and learned Minister of God's Word, and open his grief; that by the ministry of God's holy Word he may receive the benefit of absolution, together with ghostly counsel and advice, to the quieting of his conscience, and avoiding of all scruple and doubtfulness.

The Exhortation in the 1662 Book of Common Prayer

This Exhortation is uncompromising. The key to preparation

is plainly laid out: repentance, repentance, repentance, in the language of the twenty-first-century politician. Despite the archaic and exclusive language, there is very little that needs to be said about this Exhortation, which speaks for itself.

Notice how the Exhortation is not a recommendation: it is a requirement. We are required, before approaching the holy communion, to have put ourselves right with God and with our neighbour. And, if our conscience is still not quieted after this, we are to go to a priest, make our confession out loud, and receive from the priest counsel and advice and the absolution.

This may come as quite a surprise to some. The Church of England requiring this level of preparation, followed by auricular confession and absolution if self-examination is not enough to quiet the conscience?

Building on the Exhortation, the bishops whose prayers, meditations, and litanies are collected here put flesh on the bones and breathed life into these dry requirements. Using their considerable theological and pastoral experience and skill, they composed prayers, meditations, and litanies of exquisite beauty and great depth, for preparing by repentance, discernment of the body, and thanksgiving after receiving.

But, before looking at the prayers, it remains to look very briefly at the three stages of preparation: repentance, discernment, and thanksgiving, from the highly practical sermons and writings of bishops of the early Church: one each from the Roman, Greek and African Church Fathers.

Repentance: examine yourselves

St Leo the Great is famed for his practical sermons, full of good advice for his listeners. Among the finest of his sermons are those he preached during Lent, and what follows is an edited extract from a sermon he preached in Lent to the fifth-century Christians of Rome.

Brothers and sisters, so that the malice of the enemy may have no effect by its rage, a keener devotion must be awakened to the performance of the divine commands, so that we may enter into the season when all the mysteries of the divine mercy meet together, with both mind and body prepared, calling for the guidance and help of God, that we may be strong to fulfil all things through him, without whom we can do nothing.

For the injunction is laid on us, so that we may seek the aid of the one who lays it. Nor must any one excuse themselves by reason of their weakness, since he who has granted the will, also gives the power, as the blessed apostle James says: 'If any of you is lacking in wisdom, ask God, who gives to all generously and ungrudgingly, and it will be given you'.

Which of the faithful does not know what virtues they ought to cultivate, and what vices to fight against? Who is so partial or so unskilled a judge of their own conscience as not to know what ought to be removed and what ought to be developed?

Surely no one is so devoid of reason that they cannot understand the character of their way of life, or not know the secrets of their heart. Let them not then please themselves in everything, nor judge themselves according to the delights of this world, but place their every habit in the scale of the divine commands, where, some things being ordered to be done and others forbidden, they can examine themselves in a true balance by weighing the actions of their life according to this standard.

For the designing mercy of God has set up the brightest mirror in his commandments, where we may see our mind's face and realise its conformity or dissimilarity to God's image: with the specific purpose that, at least, during the days of our redemption and restoration, we may throw off for a while our worldly cares and restless occupations, and raise our thoughts from earthly matters to heavenly.

But because, as it is written, 'for all of us make many mistakes', let the feeling of mercy be first aroused and the faults of others against us be forgotten; that we may not violate by any love of revenge that most holy command, to which we bind ourselves in the Lord's prayer, when we say: 'forgive us our sins as we forgive those who sin against us'.

Let us not be hard in forgiving others. Let us not be possessed with the desire for revenge but with the leniency of gentleness. We are always exposed to the dangers of temptations and it is more desirable that our own faults should not need punishment than that we should seek to have the faults of others punished.

And what is more suitable to the Christian faith than that not only in the Church, but also in all our homes, there should be forgiveness of sins? Let threats be laid aside and let bonds be loosed, for if we do not loose them we will bind ourselves with them much more disastrously. For whatever we resolve upon against another, we decree against ourselves by our own terms.

But 'blessed are the merciful, for they will receive mercy', and he is just and kind in his judgements . . . No one should dare to refuse the pardon to another's shortcomings they wish to receive for their own.

Furthermore, as the Lord says that 'Blessed are the peacemakers, for they will be called children of God', let all discords and enmities be laid aside, and let no one think to have a share in the Paschal feast if they have neglected to restore peace with their brothers and sisters. For with the Father on high, anyone that is not in charity with their brothers and sisters, will not be reckoned in the number of his children.

Furthermore, in the distribution of charity and care of the poor . . . let each give the weak and destitute those good things they deny themselves. Let pains be taken that all may bless God with one mouth, and let the one that gives some part of their substance understand that they are a minister of the divine mercy; for God has placed the cause of the poor in the hand of the generous person, so that the sins which are washed away either by the waters of baptism or with the tears of repentance, may be also blotted out by alms-giving; for as it is written, 'As water extinguishes a blazing fire, so almsgiving atones for sin'.

Leo the Great, Sermon 49

So, self-examination is not just about feeling sorry for our sins. This is a part of the preparation required, certainly, but action must follow close on the heels of repentance. If we have fallen out with someone for some reason, if we are not in what the *Book of Common Prayer* calls 'love and charity with our neighbour', we have no place at the table. If we seek to eat and drink at the Lord's table, to feast on his good things, and we hate someone else, or have left some hurt or injury with someone, or seen someone needy and passed them by, we are deceiving ourselves if we think that we do anything other than to eat and drink our own condemnation.

Discernment: recognizing the body

What body is Paul talking about? Christ's physical body? Or his spiritual body, which is the Church? St John Chrysostom, the fourth-century Bishop of Constantinople, had this to say, when he preached one of his powerful sermons, on this passage:

Why so? Because Christ poured out his blood, and makes the thing appear a slaughter and no longer a sacrifice. Just as those who pierced him, pierced him not to drink but so they could shed his blood, anyone that comes for it unworthily does the same thing, and reaps no profit from it.

Look how frightening Paul makes his comments, and how much he rails against them, telling them that if they drink like this, they partake unworthily of the elements!

But how can it be other than unworthily if one neglects the hungry? And, on top of this, puts the hungry to shame? If not giving to the poor casts one out of the kingdom, even though one should be a virgin (or rather, not giving liberally, for even those virgins had some oil they could have given), consider how great the evil will prove, to have done something as evil as despising the poor.

'What evil?' you ask. But why do you need to ask? You have partaken of such a table as this, and when you ought to be more gentle than any, and like the angels, you become more cruel than anyone. You have tasted the blood of the Lord, and then you cannot even acknowledge your brother or sister. Of what blessing then are you worthy?

Even if you see a poor person you do not know, you should have come to the knowledge of that person from the table. But now you dishonour the table itself: Christ deemed the poor worthy to eat at his table, and you judge the poor unworthy of even a few crumbs from your food.

Have you not heard in the Gospel [Matthew 18] how much the man who demanded the hundred pence suffered? How he was forgiven the debt he owed to the master, but showed no mercy to the man who owed to him?

Have you completely lost sight of what you were and

what you have become? Have you forgotten that if a poor person is poor in possessions, you were much poorer in good works, being full of ten thousand sins?

But despite this, God delivered you from all those and counted you worthy of such a table. And you have not even become more merciful yourself: therefore, of course, nothing else remains but that you should be 'delivered to the tormentors'!

Let us listen to these words, all of us who approach with the poor to this holy table but then go out and do not seem even to have seen them, but are both drunken and callously pass by the hungry on our way home. These are the very things the Corinthians were accused of!

'And when have we done this?', I hear you say. All the time! But especially at the festivals, when above all other times it ought not to be so. Can you not see that at such times, immediately after communion, drunkenness follows, and contempt of the poor? And having partaken of the blood, when it should have been a time for you to fast and watch, you give yourself up to drink and partying . . .

Think for a minute about when the disciples ate and drank at that holy Supper, what they did: what else but prayers and singing of hymns, and sacred vigils, and teaching, all so full of self-denial? It was then that Christ related to them those great and wonderful things, when Judas had gone out to call them who were about to crucify him . . .

It is our duty to be moderate both before and after the communion, but particularly after we have received the Bridegroom. Before, that we may become worthy of receiving: after, that we may not be found unworthy of what we have received.

From St John Chrysostom, Sermon 27

In Chrysostom's time, there was a real problem with actual

drunkenness, but it does not matter whether they, or we, are drunk on the fruit of the vine, or on the wine of self-righteousness, because the end result is the same: we become insensible to those around us, we fail to see Christ in the poor, Christ in the hungry, Christ in the dispossessed, Christ in all our brothers and sisters. Then, having had our own enormous debt cancelled, and tasted of the fruits of that great act of Christ's love for us, we refuse to do the same for others. Having received the greatest possible mercy for ourselves, we show no mercy. We have condemned ourselves, literally eaten and drunk our own condemnation.

Thanksgiving: true eucharist

The holy communion is not just a memorial of Christ's passion and death. It is, at the same time, a celebration of life. A celebration of the giving of one life, and a celebration of the free gift offered to us of life for all.

Certainly, we give thanks for the saving passion, but we also give thanks for the life-giving death and resurrection of our Saviour. Christ commanded us to keep a perpetual memory of his perpetual sacrifice. As we keep this memorial, year on year, and day on day, we are kept in mind that he is in heaven, standing before his Father and offering the same life-giving sacrifice, to the end of time.

The pledges given to us, of that night in the upper room and all the wonderful events that followed, the passion, the death, the three days in the tomb, the descent into hell to free the ancient prisoners, the resurrection, the ascension, are here for us to partake in now, today, tomorrow, and as long as the earth lasts. This bread from heaven is not corruptible or withdrawn after a while like the manna our fathers ate in the desert. Neither do we, like them, eat of heavenly bread and die. No, we eat the bread of eternal life, for whoever eats this bread, prepared and worthy and discerning it for what it is, shall live for ever.

'For my flesh,' says Christ, 'is true food and my blood is true drink'. By ordinary food and drink we aim to neither be hungry nor thirsty. But nothing is able to do this except the food and drink that can make us both immortal and incorruptible. Only this food and this drink can give all of us a fellowship with the many saints, in full and perfect unity.

It is for this reason, as men and women of God have understood perfectly before us, that Christ directed our minds to his body and blood, by which many things are reduced to one thing. Consider for a moment: we partake of one bread made from many grains, and many grapes are pressed to get the one cup of wine we share . . .

Elsewhere, Christ says: 'The Father is greater than I', and this is because he was sent by the Father. And this sending is what Paul was talking about when he says that Christ emptied himself, taking the form of a servant. Though he did this in human form, he remains equal with the Father in his nature . . .

'Just as the living Father sent me,' says Christ, 'and I live because of the Father, so whoever eats me will live because of me'. Look, he does not say 'As I eat the Father and live by the Father . . . '. The Son who was created equal to the Father does not become better by eating him! But we who participate in the Son are made better through the unity of his body and blood, and this is what the eating and drinking signifies. We live by him by participating in him, by receiving him as the eternal life that we cannot otherwise have . . .

'Just as the living Father sent me,' says Christ, 'and I live because of the Father, so whoever eats me will live because of me'. What he is saying is something like: 'My emptying myself when the Father sent me means that I live by the

Father. That is, my life is in him who is greater, and those who live in me become greater too because they eat of me. If I live by the Father by being humbled, so humanity is raised up and lives by me' . . .

Here Christ explains what it really means to eat his body and drink his blood: 'I am the living bread that came down from heaven . . . Those who eat my flesh and drink my blood abide in me and I in them'. When we eat his flesh and drink his blood, it is then that we dwell in him and he dwells in us . . .

'This is the bread that came down from heaven.' By eating this bread we can have eternal life, something we could not otherwise have. 'Not like that which your ancestors ate, and they died. But the one who eats this bread shall live for ever.' Our ancestors are dead and we shall certainly die in this life, but we shall also have eternal life because Christ is eternal life.

St Augustine of Hippo, Tractate 26 on John 6

All the marvellous things that Christ did for us, he did for just one purpose: that we might have life. The life of all gave his life so that we might have life. We are freed from death's hold over us and have been offered the gift of eternal life: there is nothing, nothing at all, for which we should give thanks more than that.

I

Repentance

Repentance is the key that opens the door to a proper reception of the holy communion. It is the starting point, for any sort of worthy reception must presuppose repentance. And it is the end point, too, because it is only by repentance that we can find forgiveness.

The parable of the prodigal son is often used to illustrate repentance, a very popular motif in devotional material. Here, the father, symbolizing God, waits patiently for his repentant son to return to him. But there was a rabbinic parable that takes a very similar idea much further:

> A king had a son who had gone astray from his father by a journey of one hundred days. The son's friends said to him: 'Return to your father'. The son replied: 'I cannot'. So his father sent word to him to say: 'Then return to me as far as you can, and I will come out to meet you the rest of the way'. So God says: 'Return to me, and I will return to you'.
>
> Pes.R. 184b fin.–185a init.

None of this first part is really either designed or suitable for corporate use, especially not in church. These prayers and litanies are very personal, and are best used alone, or in very small groups, prior to any sort of liturgical expression of repentance.

A selection of prayers of repentance

O God, in whatever way I have sinned against you from my childhood even to this very moment, whether knowingly or unknowingly, within or without, sleeping or waking, in thought, word or deed, due to the fiery darts of the enemy or to the desires of my heart, take pity on me and release me, through Jesus Christ our Lord. Amen.

Laud's Private Devotions

O Lord, inasmuch as I stand before your fearful judgement-seat, where there will be no regarding of persons, I acknowledge my guilt, so let the day of my judgement come before me today. Prostrate before your holy altar, and humbled by my own conscience, in the hearing of the astounded angels before you, I reveal my impure and shameful thoughts and actions.

Laud's Private Devotions

Blessed God! How great was our misery, how great was your mercy, when nothing could save us from ruin, but the death of your Son. I see by this how hateful sin is to you. Make it hateful to me, I pray. May I never flatter myself that your mercy will spare me if I continue in sin, for you did not spare your own Son when he put himself in the place of sinners. May I never provoke your justice! May I never forget your mercies, and what your Son has done for me!

Enable me, O Lord, so to examine and to judge myself before I go to this holy sacrament, that I may not be condemned by you when you come to judge the world in righteousness. And pardon, O Lord, the many times in my life past, that I have gone to this supper without that care and devotion required of all worthy communicants, for your mercy's sake. Amen.

Wilson's Lord's Supper

Take account, I pray, Lord, of my humility, and forgive all my sins, which have been multiplied more than the hairs of my head. Forgive whatever is evil, then, and whatever I have failed to notice in my own soul, and the unpunished and unspeakable things I have done. For I am guilty, Lord, of envy, and gluttony, and all the rest.

But the multitude of your compassion is beyond compare, and the mercy of your goodness beyond describing, by which you endure my many sins. Therefore, O King greater than all wonder, O long-suffering Lord, perform the miracle of your mercies in me, a sinner. Show the power of your goodness, the depth of your love. Stretch forth your mighty arm, and receive me, a reverent prodigal, through Jesus Christ our Lord. Amen.

Laud's Private Devotions

Blessed be God, who by his grace, and by the voice of his Church, has called me to repentance! Show me, O searcher of hearts, the charge that is against me, that I may know, and confess, and forsake, the sins I have fallen into. Give me that true repentance for which you have promised mercy and pardon, that I may amend where I have done amiss, and that sin may not be my ruin.

And, O blessed Advocate, who ever lives to make intercession for us, I put my cause into your hands. Let your blood and merits plead for me, and by your mighty intercession procure for me the pardon of my past offences. Then you may say to me, as you did to the penitent in the Gospel: 'Your sins are forgiven', and I may go with a quiet conscience to your holy table. Amen.

Wilson's Lord's Supper

O Lord, I have fallen short in many things, I have acted wrongly, and caused sadness to your most Holy Spirit; I have provoked the compassion of your kindness by thought, word and deed, by night and by day, openly and in secret, intentionally and unintentionally. If you were to show me my sins, if you were to require an account from me for those sins known to you that I have committed knowingly, what should I do? Where should I hide?

But in your anger Lord, do not accuse me, nor reproach me in your wrath. Rather, pity me, not only because I am weak and sick, but because I am the work of your own hand. I beg you, do not enter into judgement with your servant, for if you, O Lord, should mark iniquities, Lord, who could stand?

Surely not I, if anyone at all. For I am adrift in a sea of sin, and am not worthy to be received into heaven on account of the multitude of my sins, which are without number, my shameful deeds, injustices and the rest, and a thousand more of the unspeakable things from which I have not left off.

By which of my sins have I not been corrupted? By which evils have I not been bound hand and foot? I have become unprofitable to you, my God, and to all humanity. Who, having fallen under such a weight of sin, can ever stand again?

But in you, Lord, I trust, a loving God; be for me a Saviour according to the depths of your compassion. Pity me according to your great mercy, and do not pay me back according to my works, but turn yourself to me, and me to you. Remit all my sins against you, save me by your mercy, and where sin abounds, let your grace abound all the more, and I shall praise and glorify you all the days of my life.

For you are the God of the penitent and the Saviour of those who sin, and to you be glory, through Jesus Christ our Lord. Amen.

Laud's Private Devotions

Bishop Brian Duppa's Guide for the Penitent

Righteousness, O Lord, belongs to you; but to me belongs confusion and sorrow, for I am the vainest, the vilest, the most sinful of all your children. Lord, I am vile in my own eyes, and I will be yet more vile, because my sins have made me vile in yours.

I am not worthy of the air I breathe, of the earth I tread upon, or of the sun that shines on me. How much less worthy, then, to lift up either hands or eyes to heaven? For you have said that no unclean thing shall come within your sight: how then shall I appear before your presence, who am so miserably defiled?

If David, the 'man according to your own heart', could say that he was a 'worm and no man', O Lord, what am I?

And if the righteous Abraham, who had the honour to be called your friend, could say that he was 'but dust and ashes', O Lord, what am I?

O my God, you made me out of nothing; and you see how I have spoiled this work of yours, for I have made myself worse than nothing. I am utterly consumed by my sins, and do not know what to do.

But this much I can do:

I will confess my wickedness, and be sorry for my sins. I will stand apart with the publican, and strike my breast, and say, 'Lord, be merciful to me a sinner'.

I will return with the prodigal son, and say, 'Father, I am not worthy to be called your son; make me as one of your hired servants'.

I will not 'suffer my eyes to sleep, nor my eyelids to slumber', until, by the mediation of your dear Son, I have obtained my pardon.

And what more can I say? I will pour out my prayers in the

bitterness of my spirit; and if my dry eyes lack tears, I will call on my heart for tears of blood with which I may supply them.

And now, Lord, make me remember my sins: and when you have done so, blot them out of your book, and pardon me.

A litany of confession

Woe to me, O God, that being one of your creatures, the work of your hands, and capable of enjoying everlasting happiness, I have lived so poorly and wickedly that unless your mercy prevents it I shall utterly lose the true end of my creation.

But I repent, O my God, I repent. I am utterly ashamed of it. Lord, be merciful to me a sinner.

Woe to me, O God, that I have frittered away so many of my youngest days without knowing you, or taking any notice of those strict duties that I owe to you. Woe to me that I was so long a child in everything except innocence.

But I repent, O my God, I repent. I accuse and judge and condemn myself for it. Lord, be merciful to me a sinner.

Woe to me, O God, that as I grew up, the seeds of corruption which I brought with me into the world grew up along with me, and by small degrees, which I did not even notice, pride and foolishness took hold of me, and sin has reigned in my mortal body.

But I repent, O my God, I repent. I am infinitely confounded at it. Lord, be merciful to me a sinner.

Woe to me, O God, that being washed in the waters of baptism from the guilt of that original corruption that I brought with me into the world, I have since that time so defiled myself that I can no longer pretend that I have any contract with you: that

I am either a child of yours, a member of your Christ, or an heir of the kingdom of heaven.

But I repent, O my God, I repent. I am utterly confounded at it. Lord, be merciful to me a sinner.

Woe to me, O God, that having been received into the bosom of your Church, which so many millions of souls have not had the happiness to be, I have ungratefully dishonoured your holy faith by an unholy life; and having so often confessed you with my tongue, I have denied you in my life and my actions.

But I repent, O my God, I repent. I accuse and judge and condemn myself for it. Lord, be merciful to me a sinner.

Woe to me, O God, that having rejected the devil and all his works, and given up my name to Christ, to fight under the banner of his cross, I have on the contrary treacherously complied with his enemy in many things, and shall be found, I fear, to have been more diligent in serving the enemy than I have ever been in serving you.

But I repent, O my God, I repent. I am confounded and astonished at it. Lord, be merciful to me a sinner.

Woe to me, O God, that being obliged by that high calling of being a Christian to renounce the pomps and vanities of the world, I have so infinitely failed in this that I have longed and worked for nothing more than what I claim to have renounced: those very vanities have been my idols, and my seduced heart has gone running after them.

But I repent, O my God, I repent. I am utterly confounded at it. Lord, be merciful to me a sinner.

Woe to me, O God, that being further bound by a most solemn vow to utterly forsake the sinful lusts of the flesh, I have, instead of forsaking them, pursued and hunted after them; and

when other temptations have failed, have been quick enough
to kindle my own fire, and to be a tempter to myself.

*But I repent, O my God, I repent. I hate and loathe and
despise myself for it. Lord, be merciful to me a sinner.*

Woe to me, O God, that knowing your revealed will to be the
law to which I was bound in all obedience to submit myself,
I, like an insolent rebel, have not only set up my own will in
opposition to yours, but have many times preferred my own
will to yours, and have listened more to the false words of flesh
and blood than to any of your holy commandments.

*But I repent, O my God, I repent. I am utterly confounded
at it. Lord, be merciful to me a sinner.*

Woe to me, O God, that being made in your image, the greatest honour for any creature, I have obscured it with so many
blurs and spots and foul sins, so defaced all the lines and fea-
tures of it, that unless your Holy Spirit renews that image in
me again, I tremble to think what I must one day hear: 'Depart
from me, I do not know you'.

*But I repent, O my God, I repent. I am ashamed and
confounded at it. Lord, be merciful to me a sinner.*

Woe to me, O God, that having received a rational soul from
you to be a moral light and guide for my actions, I have been so
brutish as to follow my sensual appetite instead of it, and have
made no further use of reason than to discover vain excuses to
encourage my own soul down the road of sin and error.

*But I repent, O my God, I repent. I accuse and judge and
condemn myself for it. Lord, be merciful to me a sinner.*

Woe to me, O God, that being blessed with memory to serve

as a storehouse in which to treasure your words and your holy commandments, I have stuffed it so miserably full with vanities and sins that I have no room left for you at all.

But I repent, O my God, I repent. I infinitely condemn myself for it. Lord, be merciful to me a sinner.

Woe to me, O God, that having received a heart from you to be the seat of clean and holy thoughts and the temple for your Holy Spirit to dwell in, I have so unworthily abused and corrupted it, that it is now become a den of thieves, and an ugly vessel of all uncleanness.

But I repent, O my God, I repent. I hate and loathe and abhor myself for it. Lord, be merciful to me a sinner.

Woe to me, O God, that my wretched heart being corrupted, my imagination has run wildly after it with a swarm of vain and sinful thoughts, which like flies being driven away settle again and again upon my distracted soul, and intermingle with the best of my intentions.

But I repent, O my God, I repent. I am infinitely troubled and grieved for it. Lord, be merciful to me a sinner.

Woe to me, O God, that my eyes being greedy for the things of this world, have been permanently open windows to let in sin; but while they should have cried penitential tears to wash away the stains those sins had made, there has been no way out for them.

But I repent, O my God, I repent. I am inwardly grieved and deplore myself for it. Lord, be merciful to me a sinner.

Woe to me, O my God, that for hearing useless conversation I have left my ears open to light and vain and sinful words, and all my life have listened more to what the world says than to what your Holy Spirit and my own conscience say within me.

But I repent, O my God, I repent. I accuse and judge and condemn myself for it. Lord, be merciful to me a sinner.

Woe to me, O God, that I have not resolved like your servant David to take care of my ways, that I do not offend with my tongue, but many times have inconsiderately let it loose; and, either to please the company I am with or my own self, I have spoken words which might unhappily prove occasions of sin both to them and to me, without regard to the great flames that such little sparks might kindle.

But I repent, O my God, I repent. I do infinitely condemn myself for it. Lord, be merciful to me a sinner.

Woe to me, O God, that all the parts and faculties of my soul and body have been abused, and have not served the laws of their creator, but have so eagerly and constantly gone after the corrupt desires of a seduced heart, that I have cause to fear that either my whole life may be looked upon as one continuous sin, or at least as having had so few pauses that if you were to enter into strict judgement with me, I should not have the confidence to say when or where or how I have ever been innocent.

But I repent, O my God, I repent. I am confounded and astonished at it. Lord, be merciful to me a sinner.

Woe to me, O God, that I have wretchedly failed even in my best efforts; that I have been cold in my devotions, weary of my prayers, resistant to good purposes, dull and heavy in the way to heaven, but quick and active in all the ways of sin, having made it the whole business of my life, rather to appear to be religious than to really be so.

But I repent, O my God, I repent. I accuse and judge and condemn myself for it. Lord, be merciful to me a sinner.

Woe to me, O God, that I have not washed my hands in innocency when I have gone up to your altar, nor made my heart ready to receive the bread that came from heaven, but have failed in my preparations, and have not sufficiently considered either my own unworthiness or the deep secrets of so great a mystery.

But I repent, O my God, I repent. I am grieved and troubled at it. Lord, be merciful to me a sinner.

Woe to me, O God, that having so often received those inestimable pledges of your love, the precious body and blood of your dear Son in the holy sacrament, I have been so unwary as to let in my former sins under the same roof with you, and have unhappily done whatever I could to drive you from me.

But I repent, O my God, I repent. I am infinitely ashamed at it. Lord, be merciful to me a sinner.

Woe to me, O God, that my repentance, the only plank left for me in the shipwreck of my soul, has been so weak, so slight, and so unsteady, that every small blast of a new temptation has been able to drive me from it, and by frequent relapses into sin makes me want to repent even of my own pitiful repentance.

But I repent again, O God, again I repent. I hate and loathe and abhor myself for it. Lord, be merciful to me a sinner.

Woe to me, O God, that having received my life and being and continued existence from you, with so many advantages that have made me happy in this world and blessed in the next, I have been so abominably unthankful that I have cast all your blessings behind me and returned you nothing for all your favours but insults, and injuries, and sins.

But I repent, O God, I repent. I am confounded and astonished at it. Lord, be merciful to me a sinner.

Woe to me, O God, that being redeemed by the death and passion and glorious resurrection of your dear and only Son, I have not taken his bitter agonies to heart, nor made right use of the precious ransom which was paid for me; that I have not yet worked out my pardon with such penitent tears as you require, nor laid hold of the benefits of it by a lively faith; but have chosen rather stupidly to continue in my sins, and to neglect the blood of the covenant as though it was an unholy thing.

But I repent, O my God, I repent. I hate and loathe and abhor myself for it. Lord, be merciful to me a sinner.

Woe to me, O God, that I have grieved your Holy Spirit, rejected your counsels, quenched your actions within me, and have entertained the lusts and vanities of this life with far more care and passionate affection then any of your holy inspirations.

But I repent, O my God, I repent. I am utterly ashamed and confounded at it. Lord, be merciful to me a sinner.

Woe to me, O God, that having so opened my guilty heart before you I have left so many sins behind that I cannot number them; some that I have really forgotten, some I would much rather forget if my conscience would let me; open sins that I cannot conceal, and secret sins that I have taken so much care to hide from others that they have become hidden even from myself.

But whatever these sins may be, or wherever they are recorded, whether in my own conscience or in any other place, that may be used against me on the day of judgement, I call the whole company of heaven to witness: that I sadly repent myself of them all; that I abhor myself for them all; that I resolve steadfastly to renounce them all. Lord, be merciful to me a sinner. Amen and amen.

The penitent's prayer

O God the Father, who cannot be thought so cruel as to create me only to destroy me: have mercy on me.

O God the Son, who knowing your Father's will, made it your business to come into the world to save me: have mercy on me.

O God the Holy Spirit, who to save me have sanctified me in my baptism, and have so often since breathed holy thoughts and intentions into me: have mercy on me.

O holy and blessed and glorious Trinity, who in three persons I adore as my one and only true God: have mercy on me; hear me, O Lord; help me, O Lord; save me, or else I shall surely die.

O Lord, do you not care that I perish; you who will that all shall be saved; you who would rather that none should perish? And will you now show your anger against a worm, against a leaf blown about in the wind, against a vapour that vanishes before you? Remember how short my time is, and do not deliver my soul into the power of hell. For what profit is there in my blood? Or who shall praise you in that bottomless pit?

No, let me live in your sight. Let me live, O my God, that my soul may praise you. Forget me as I have been, disobedient and provoking you to anger, and remember me as I am, distressed and crying out to you for help. Do not look on me as I am, a sinner, but consider me as I am, your creature and the work of your hands.

O Lord, I confess that I am a sinner, and a sinner of no ordinary sort; but do not let this hinder you, O my God, for in the repentance of such sinners you take the greatest pleasure.

Remember for whose sake it was that you came from the bosom of your Father, and let yourself down so low as to be content to be born of your own humble handmaid. Remember for who it was that your tender body was torn, and scourged, and crucified, and your precious blood was shed.

Was it not for the sins of the whole world? And shall I be so narrow-hearted to my own soul, or so injurious to your glory, as to think that in all this crowd you have particularly excepted me? Or, which is as great a dishonour to you, can I possibly imagine that you died only for sinners of a lower kind even than me, and left such as I am without remedy?

If that was the case, what would have become then of him who filled Jerusalem with blood? What of the noted woman who had lived in a trade of sin? No, Lord, what would have become of your own disciple who with oaths and curses denied you three times?

Oh, how easy is it for you to forgive, for it is your nature. How proper is it for you to save, for it is your name. How suitable is it to your reason for coming into the world, for that was your business. And when I consider that I am the chief of sinners, may I not urge the Father, and say, 'Shall the very chief of your business be left undone?' Mercy! Mercy, good Lord!

I do not ask of you the things of this world: neither power, nor honours, nor riches, nor pleasures. No, my God, give them to whoever you please, but give me mercy.

Oh, that I could hear you say to me, as you said to the one in the Gospel, 'My child, be of good cheer, for your sins are forgiven'.

How would my drooping spirits revive at such a sound? And how would my now wounded soul break forth into psalms and hymns and spiritual songs for a mercy so utterly undeserved, and that the angels which fell could never hear of?

But, O my weak soul, what do you fear? Why do you shake? For you are not yet in such a desperate condition, and what was said to him may possibly still be said to you. No, be confident, though it be with a mixture of fear and trembling, that if you do not act the part of a hypocrite all this while, your

Saviour stands ready at the doors of your heart, to breathe the very same words in a heavenly whisper to you: 'Be of good cheer, for your sins are forgiven'.

Duppa's Guide for the Penitent

2

Discernment

Having asked forgiveness of God, and anyone we have need of asking forgiveness of, the next stage of a proper preparation is discernment. We must both know what it is we are about to receive and also why we are receiving it. We must discern the body, as Paul would say: not just Christ's body in the holy communion, but also his wider body, the Church, and also in the widest possible sense of all his creation.

O God, our Father in heaven, who have given over your only-begotten Son to death for us;

O Son, redeemer of the world, God, who have washed us by your precious blood;

O Holy Spirit, Comforter, God, who by your grace have visited and strengthened the hearts of your saints;

O Most Holy, highest, everlasting Trinity, blest and worthy of blessing: good Father, devout Son and kindly Spirit; whose work is life, love, grace, contemplation and glory; whose majesty is unspeakable, whose power incomparable, and goodness inestimable; who, at the same time is Lord both of the living and of the dead: I adore you, I call upon you, and with every beat of my heart I bless you, now and to the ages. Amen.

Laud's Private Devotions

O Lord, I am not worthy, I am not fit, that you should come under the roof of my soul; for it is all desolate and ruined;

nor have you in me a fitting place to lay your head. But, as you condescended to lie in the cavern and manger of brute cattle, as you did not disdain to be entertained in the house of Simon the leper, as you did not repel that harlot, like me, who was a sinner, coming to you and touching you; as you did not despise her polluted and loathsome mouth; nor the thief upon the cross confessing you: so me too the ruined, wretched, and excessive sinner, allow to receive, to touch, and partake of the immaculate, supernatural, life-giving, and saving mysteries of your all-holy body and your precious blood.

Listen, O Lord our God, from your holy habitation, and from the glorious throne of your kingdom, and come to sanctify us. You who sit on high with the Father, and are invisibly present with us here: come to sanctify the gifts which lie before you, and those on whose behalf, and by whom, and the things for which, they are brought near you. And grant to us communion, unto faith without shame, love without fading or ending, fulfilment of your commandments, zeal for every spiritual fruit, hindrance of all adversity, healing of soul and body; that we too, with all the saints who have been well-pleasing to you from the beginning, may become partakers of the incorruptible and everlasting things that you have prepared, O Lord, for those who love you, and in whom you are glorified for ever and ever. Amen.

Andrewes' Private Devotions

O Lord Jesus, give to the living mercy and grace, and to those you have taken for yourself guidance and light perpetual; give to your Church truth and peace; and give to me, the most wretched of sinners, repentance and pardon. Amen.

Laud's Private Devotions

O Lord, I pray you, correct those who are erring, convert the unbelievers, increase the Church in faith, destroy heresies,

disclose our sly opponents, restrain the violent and unrepent-
ant, through Jesus Christ our Lord. Amen.

Laud's Private Devotions

O my most blessed Saviour, who in the depths of your mercy
towards humanity not only offered yourself as a sacrifice for
the sins of the whole world, but instituted this heavenly and
holy sacrament as the means to convey the benefits of your
precious death to all who come to you in humility and repentance: accept, I pray, this my humble prayer, as I present myself
before you as a useless sinner I confess, but one who is heartily
sorry for my sins and penitent for my offences.

Direct me therefore, my God, in this great work of yours,
with such a reverent and aweful fear that all the faculties of
my soul may be attentive, to rightly understand and joyfully
receive this most wonderful mystery of your body and blood.

O my Lord, I am not worthy that you should come under
my roof; therefore before you come again as judge, let your
Holy Spirit prepare and dress up a place for you in my soul,
cleansing it from the stains of sin, and permitting nothing to
remain in it to keep you out; so that being wholly possessed by
you, all sinful thoughts and unclean suggestions may not only
disappear, but never find a place in me again.

Grant this, my Jesus, and so this day receive me into your
favour, that with joy I may receive you into my soul, and once
I am united with you never let your grace depart from me, so
you may live in me and I in you for ever. Amen.

Duppa's Holy Rules and Helps

Lamb of God, that take away the sin of the world, take away
the sins of me, the utter sinner.

So we, too, O sovereign Lord, remembering in the presence
of your holy mysteries the health-giving passion of your Christ
and his life-giving cross, his most precious death, his three days

in the tomb, his resurrection from the dead, his ascent into heaven, his taking his seat at your right hand, O Lord; grant that we, receiving in the pure testimony of our conscience, our portion of your sacred things, may be made one with the holy body and blood of your Christ; and not receiving them unworthily may hold Christ indwelling in our hearts, and may become a temple of your Holy Spirit.

Yes, our God, and do not make any of us guilty of your dreadful and heavenly mysteries, nor infirm in soul or body from partaking of them unworthily. But grant us until our last and closing breath, worthily to receive a hope of your holy things, for sanctification, enlightening, strengthening, a relief of the weight of many sins, a preservative against all workings of the devil, a riddance and hindrance of evil conscience, a mortification of passions, a taking-hold of your commandments, an increase of your divine grace, and a securing of your kingdom. Amen.

Andrewes' Private Devotions

Blessed Lord Jesus! I even tremble when I remember that whoever eats and drinks unworthily is guilty of your body and blood, and eats and drinks damnation to their own soul, and this severe sentence on unworthy communicants makes me afraid to come to your altar.

But when I remember that your sentence is as severe against those who are invited but refuse to come, for you have said they shall not taste of your supper, and unless we eat your flesh and drink your blood we have no life in us, I am afraid to stay away.

But blessed be your mercy O Lord, for this is the state my soul is in: you are my guide and by giving me this opportunity of receiving, invite me to your table. You call me to seek your face and my heart replies: 'Your face, Lord, will I seek!'

If you, Lord, should be extreme to mark what is done amiss, alas, for I am then unfit not only to communicate, but to say even my daily prayers.

I know, Lord, that if I stay away until I am worthy to come, then I shall never come. And though I am unworthy of so unspeakable a mercy, yet I come, begging your grace to make me worthy, or at least such as you will accept!

O blessed Jesus, open my eye of faith, so as to discern your body and blood in the holy sacrament. Make my soul long for this communion, that I may feel all the happy effects of your own divine institution, that my soul may receive such lasting impressions of your goodness, and be so filled with the love of you, and with the incomparable delights of your service, and with such an early foretaste of heaven, that all the pleasures of sin which tempt me may appear to me tasteless and unwelcome.

O heavenly Father, clothe me with the wedding garment, the graces of my blessed Saviour, for then am I sure to be a welcome guest at your table, when I shall approach in the likeness of your only well-beloved Son, in whom you are always well-pleased!

O heavenly Father, fill me with a lively faith, profound humility, the obedience of a child, inflamed affections, and love for all. O grant to my soul all those heavenly gifts: of zeal and devotion, of love and desire, of joy and delight, of praise and thanksgiving, suitable for the remembrance of a crucified Saviour, for one redeemed by the blood of God. And all this for his sake only, for the one that redeemed me and in whose holy words I sum up all the graces and blessings I stand in need of: Our Father . . .

Ken's Manual of prayers

O Jesus, you have loved us, and washed us from our sins, and purchased us by your own blood, and ordained this sacrament in order to secure us to yourself: by a grateful remembrance of what you have done and suffered for us make me truly aware of your love, and of our sad condition that required such a sacrifice.

May I always receive this pledge of your love, the gifts of mercy and pardon and grace offered to us in this holy supper, with a thankful heart, and in remembrance of you, our great and best benefactor; in remembrance of your holy example, of your heavenly doctrine, of your laborious life, of your bitter passion and death, of your glorious resurrection, of your ascension into heaven, and of your coming again to judge the world!

And may I never forget the obligations you have laid on us: to live lives worthy of your disciples and to turn back from every course of life contrary to your gospel. Cease not, O Lord, to love us; and by the grace given in this supper cause us to love you with all our hearts. Amen.

Wilson's Lord's Supper

Lord, what am I that you should be gracious to me? What an honour it is that I am invited here to feast at your table on the body and blood of my blessed Saviour!

What an honour to receive the pledges of his love and to join my love with his, something I want to grow more and more, as well as to increase my love for my Christian brothers and sisters and to all humanity.

I believe, O Lord, that you are the bread that came down from heaven, by which we are nourished to eternal life. And I thank you with all my soul that you have both taught us the way of truth in God and also died for our sins and risen again to give us a hope of that immortal life.

Blessed be your name, for I am about, by your own invitation, to receive the sacred pledge and earthly sign of that life. So my soul magnifies the Lord, and my spirit rejoices in God my Saviour. His grace, I trust, will be with my spirit, that I may rejoice in the Lord always, and delight only in doing good. Amen.

Patrick's Book for Beginners

Father of mercy, for the kindness shown to me on earth by my benefactors, may an eternal reward follow for them in heaven. I pray also that for those for whom I have prayed, and for those for whom I am obliged to pray, and the whole people of God, that it may be given to us to be led into your kingdom, and there to appear in justice and to be satisfied with glory; through Jesus Christ our Lord. Amen.

Laud's Private Devotions

O Lord, you who sit beside the Father, and yet invisibly return among mortals, come now and sanctify these holy gifts with your presence; for whom, by whom, and on behalf of whom they are offered. Amen.

Laud's Private Devotions

I thank you, O Lord of heaven and earth, that you have condescended to take on our nature, and in a body like ours to suffer for our sins. Yes, even to shed your most precious blood on the cross for our redemption. Glory and honour and blessing and praise to you, O Lord!

To you and not to myself should I live from this day on. And so I now devote myself to your faithful service, and resolve, if need be, even to take up my own cross and follow you. Assist me, good Lord, and make me a partaker of all the benefits of your death and passion . . . Amen.

Patrick's Book for Beginners

Grant, O God, that I may never draw down your judgements on myself, either by turning my back on this supper or by going to it without thought and unworthily. May your mercy pardon what is past, and give me grace for the time to come: to consecrate my life to you, and to embrace every occasion of remembering my Redeemer's love, and so securing your favour and my own salvation! And if it be your will, grant that I may always find such comfort and benefit in this supper as may encourage me to observe it with joy to my life's end.

Permit me to bring before your infinite mercy the miserable condition of all of us who neglect so great a means of grace and salvation. Awaken all Christian people into a sense of this duty. Open their eyes and correct their mistakes, that they may be convinced that this is the only means of making their peace with you, and of making their persons and their prayers acceptable to your divine majesty, through Jesus Christ our Lord. Amen.

Wilson's Lord's Supper

O Lamb of God, who offered yourself a sacrifice for the sins of the whole world, have mercy on me a miserable sinner. I am ready to renew the covenant I made with you in baptism, and once more to take those solemn promises on myself. O give me the assistance of your grace and your Holy Spirit, that I may be enabled to perform what I promised: that from now on I may renounce the devil and all his works, all the pomps and vanities of the world and the sinful lusts of the flesh, that I may always persist in the true faith of your most holy religion, and live in sincere obedience to your laws all the days of my life. Amen.

Anonymous Guide to Young Communicants

Grant, O Lord, I pray, that the wine that makes glad and the bread of life may infuse new strength and vitality into my soul, and into the souls of all that communicate with me, that we may daily grow in grace and in the knowledge of our Lord and Saviour Jesus Christ; and that according to his command, we may be united in holy love and fellowship with one another and with the Church of God; and at the last we may obtain that glorious fellowship with you in heaven which you have promised to all that love and fear you; through the same Jesus Christ our Lord. Amen.

Anonymous Guide to Young Communicants

Most great and incomprehensible Lord God! Truly you are worthy of all praise, and infinitely to be admired for your grace and mercy in the redemption of the world by the body and blood of your Son, whom you have given to be meat and drink for those who fear and obey you. O Lord, I intend today to eat of the bread and drink of the cup that nourishes the soul of all true penitents.

Lord, let the inward and spiritual grace accompany the holy bread and wine, that my body not only may be refreshed but also my soul refreshed and comforted and strengthened; that I may ever more continue obedient to you, blessed Jesus.

O Lord, I pray, send forth your light and your truth to guide and direct me. Establish me with your good Spirit, that you freely give to those that ask in faith; that blessed Spirit that makes our meditations of you to be sweet, yes sweeter even than milk and honey; it makes the soul rejoice more than in plenty of corn and wine and oil. This same Spirit that gave strength to overcome to the three children in the fiery furnace; to Daniel in the lions' den; to St Peter in crucifixion; to St John in the pot of boiling oil; to St Bartholomew as his skin was flayed.

Blessed God, let my heart be turned to you, and then shall I receive strength and nourishment of soul to everlasting life.

All of which I beg through the merits of Jesus Christ our Saviour, to whom with the Father and the Holy Spirit be all glory and praise, now and to the ages. Amen.

Anonymous Guide to Young Communicants

O Jesus, be a saviour to me, and let this sacrament be a foretaste of life, and the holy body and bread of life, and your precious blood the purifier of my sinful life.

Grant that I may receive these holy mysteries for the amendment of my life, a preservative against my sins, and for the increase of virtue and holiness in my soul.

Grant that being sacramentally communicated, I may derive from you grace for the amendment of my life, spiritual wisdom to see the ways of peace, the spirit of love and purity, so that in all my life I may walk in a way worthy of your gracious favour. Grant that I may do all my works in holiness and righteousness, that I may resist every temptation with a never-failing courage, and never be surprised or deceived by my spiritual enemy. Amen.

Anonymous, The Divine Banquet

Sweetest Saviour, I come to you by your invitation and commandment, without which I could never come. Do not let me go away from you any more, but enter into my heart, feed me with your Word, sustain me with your Spirit, and refresh me with your comfort. In this holy mystery, let me receive you my dearest Saviour, and be my wisdom, my righteousness, my sanctification, and my redemption.

Let me receive this holy food as a foretaste of an eternal inheritance, a defence against spiritual danger, an incentive to holy love, and a strengthening of my faith. And grant, Lord, that with you at one with me, and I at one with you, I may be found gracious in the eyes of your heavenly Father, and may receive an inheritance with the saints in light, which you have already purchased with your blood and prepared for those who love you. Amen.

Anonymous, The Divine Banquet

3

Thanksgiving

It is no accident that the service in which remembrance is made and our gifts of bread and wine are consecrated and returned to us as the body and blood of Christ in the holy communion is called Eucharist: the Greek verb *eucharistein* means to give thanks, and this sense of gratitude for every blessing we receive overflows from this selection of prayers for use after receiving the holy communion.

O Lord, the only spring and everlasting fountain of all good, who today have revived and given life to my poor soul by giving yourself to me in a wonderful way in this blessed sacrament, I praise and glorify your holy name for this your infinite mercy, begging you to crown what you have begun by a continual supply of heavenly grace, so that I may never forget who or what I have received; but being purified by your blood and strengthened by your body against all future temptations, I may constantly run through all the parts of a holy life, to the possession of your glorious kingdom, world without end. Amen.

Laud's Private Devotions

It is finished and done, so far as in our power, O Christ our God, the mystery of your dispensation. For we have held remembrance of your death, we have seen the figure of your resurrection, we have been filled with your endless life, we have enjoyed your precious gifts; graciously give to all of us in the world to come. Amen.

The things I believe to have been done for me, that I call to remembrance, for which I return thanks, that I remember and commemorate, that I offer and I pray you to offer, of all these things, Lord, make me a partaker, and apply them to me.

By the things you did and bore for us, your oblation and sacrifice, your emptying yourself, your humbling yourself, your incarnation, your conception, your birth, your circumcision (the first-fruits of your blood), your baptism, your fasting, your temptation, your homelessness, your hunger, your weariness, your thirst, your sleeplessness, your injuries, your patience and endurance, your being taken as a thief and bound, by Gethsemane, Gabbatha, Golgotha, your obedience to death, your endurance on the cross: Lord, let my prayer ascend, and do not turn your ear from me.

As you delivered our fathers, deliver us, O Lord: as you delivered Noah from the flood, Abraham from Ur of the Chaldees, Isaac from sacrifice, Lot from Sodom, Jacob from Laban and Esau, Joseph from his tempting mistress and from prison, Job from temptation, Moses from Pharaoh and from stoning, your people from the Red Sea and from Babylon, David from Saul and Goliath, Elias from Jezebel, Hezekiah from sickness, Esther from Haman, Jeremiah from the pit, the three holy children from the furnace, Jonah from the belly of the whale, the disciples from the storm, Peter from Herod's prison, Paul from shipwreck and stoning and evil beasts; even so deliver us, O Lord, that put our trust in you! Amen.

Andrewes' Private Devotions

Let all your works praise you, O Lord, and your saints give thanks to you. It is a good thing to give thanks to the Lord, to sing praises to your name, O most high, to tell of your loving-kindness in the morning and of your truth in the night. I will exalt you, my God and King, and praise your name for ever and ever. Every day will I give thanks to you, and praise your name for ever and ever.

For you have called things into being, and by you were all things made in heaven and in earth, visible and invisible. You uphold all things by the Word of your power . . . you fill our hearts with joy and gladness . . . and all things serve you.

For you, with your own hands, made our father Adam from the dust of the earth, and breathed into his nostrils the breath of life. You honoured him by making him in your own image, and instructed your angels concerning him. You set him over the work of your hands, and placed him in a Paradise of pleasure.

And you did not despise him, even when he despised your covenant, but you opened for him and for his descendants the door to repentance and life, giving him the great and precious promise concerning the seed of the woman, who would crush the head of the serpent, our ancestral enemy.

For you have instructed our race with the things you permit to be made known about you: by what was written in the Law, by the rites of Sacrifice, the oracles of the Prophets, the melody of the Psalms, the wisdom of the Proverbs, the experience of the Histories.

And, when the fullness of time was come, you sent your Son, who took the seed of Abraham, and made himself of no reputation, taking the form of a servant, and was born of a woman, born under the Law.

And who by the offering of his life fulfilled the Law, and by the sacrifice of his death removed the curse of the Law. He redeemed our race by his passion, and enlivened us by his resurrection. There was nothing that could have been done that he did not do to make us partakers of the divine nature.

He made plain in every place the truth of his knowledge: by

the preaching of the gospel, to which he himself bore witness with signs and wonders, by the holiness of his life, by mighty power even to the shedding of his blood for us . . .

He granted to his Church that she should be the pillar and foundation of truth, and that the gates of hell should not prevail against her. He granted to our Church to keep what was committed to her and to teach the way of peace.

He confirmed the throne of his servant, our ruler. He makes peace in our borders and fills us with the flour of wheat. He made fast the bars of our gates and has blessed our children within us. He has clothed our enemies with confusion. He gives us everlasting blessings and makes us glad with the joy of his face . . .

And he has brought me forth into life, and led me to the waters of regeneration and filled me with the Holy Spirit. He has overlooked my sins because he knew I would repent again . . .

He has not allowed my heart to harden, but has left me a softness of soul, a remembrance of my end, and knowledge of the sins I have committed. He has opened for me a gate of hope, as long as I confess and beg his mercy, through the power of his mysteries and the keys to loose my sins.

He has not cut off my life like a weaver, or made an end of me from day to night. He has not taken me away in the midst of my days, but has kept my soul in life and has not suffered my foot to slip. He has heard my prayer and accepted my repentance. He has given me a foretaste of his heavenly things and has saved me. Praise be to him! Amen.

Andrewes' Private Devotions

Blessed are you, O Lord . . . who according to your great mercy have made me to be born again to a lively hope by the resurrection of Jesus Christ, to an incorruptible and undefiled inheritance that will not fade away, reserved for me in heaven.

You have blessed me with every spiritual blessing in heavenly things in Christ. You comfort me in my trouble, so that as the passions of Christ grow in me, my hope and help should also grow through Christ.

I give you thanks, O God of my fathers. I praise you, who have given me some measure of wisdom and courage, and have showed to me what I requested of you, and have opened my mouth.

You have made me the work of your hands and the price of your blood, the image of your divinity and the servant of your great purchase, the seal of your name and a child by adoption, the temple of your Holy Spirit and a member of your Christ! Amen.

Andrewes' Private Devotions

Glory be to you O Jesus, my Lord and my God, for feeding my soul with your most blessed body and blood. O let your heavenly food transfuse new life and new vigour into my soul, and into the souls of all that communicate with me, that our faith may daily increase, that we may all grow more humble and contrite for our sins, that we may all love you and serve you and delight in you, and praise you more fervently, more incessantly, then ever we have done before! Amen and amen.

Ken's Manual of Prayers

O how plentiful is your goodness, my Lord and my God, which you have laid up for those that fear you, which you have promised for those that put their trust in your mercy!

Was it not love infinite enough, dearest Lord, to give yourself for me on the cross? Was not that sacrifice of yourself sufficient to pay for the sins of the whole world? What more, Lord, could you do for me?

All the mighty host of heaven stood amazed to see the blood of God shed, to see their King of Glory, to whom from everlasting they had sung their hymns of praise, nailed to a cross; and all this to save sinners!

Surely, Lord, none of all those blessed spirits, with all the glorious illuminations they had, could ever have imagined how you could give yourself more to us than you have done.

And yet despite all this you have worked new miracles of love for us. And as if it had not been love enough to have given yourself for us on the cross, you have made a way to give yourself to us in the holy sacrament; to unite yourself to us with the most intimate union that it is possible to imagine; to become the food, the life, the strength, the support, of my soul; to become one with me, to become the very soul of my soul!

O Lord God, this is so inconceivable a blessing, this is so divine a union, that the very angels who so much desire to look into the great mystery of our redemption, who learn your manifold wisdom from your Church, and visit the places of your worship, who crowd about our altars, stand with awe-filled admiration as they contemplate this holy sacrament!

What thanks, then, gracious Lord, can I return to you for those wonders of love you have shown to me, a wretched sinner, which the angels themselves, who never sinned, so much admire?

O dearest Lord, raise up my devotion to the highest pitch it can possibly reach, to praise you; enlarge my soul to its utmost extent, to love you!

How can I ever more offend such riches of mercy as are in you, O crucified Saviour? And yet while I carry this body of sin about me I fear I shall. But, Lord, from my heart I renounce and hate all the things that displease you; I resolve to the utmost of my power to resist all temptations, and to become as totally yours as my frail nature will permit me.

O gracious Lord, who has so infinitely loved us and given us everlasting consolation and good hope through grace, comfort my heart and for ever establish it in every good word and work!

Blessing, and honour, and glory, and power, be to him that sits on the throne, and to the Lamb for ever!

Rejoice in the Lord Jesus, O my soul, for of him comes my salvation.

I will love you, O Lord my King, and I will praise your name for ever and ever!

Glory be to you, O Lord God, for giving me this blessed opportunity of coming to your altar! O grant I may never more pollute my soul, that you have now made your temple to reside in, you who are the God of purity!

Praise the Lord O my soul, while I live will I praise the Lord; as long as I have any being I will sing praises to you, O blessed Saviour, my King, and my God.

O gracious Lord, pardon all my failings, accept all my prayers and praises, and supply all my needs, that I sum up in your own blessed words: Our Father . . .

Ken's Manual of Prayers

Blessed be the Lord for his exceedingly great grace and mercy to us in Christ Jesus!

Blessed be the Lord who has called me into fellowship with him and with his Son Jesus Christ!

Blessed be his name, for I have now received the tokens of his endless love, in which I ought to rejoice without ceasing, and hold as more valuable than all the things of this world!

It is my joy, O Lord, my highest satisfaction in this world, to know I am beloved of you, who are able to make me happier than it is possible to conceive. O keep me for ever in your love, and to that end preserve in me the same thoughts, resolutions and devout affections that I now feel in my heart.

Keep them alive by the powerful help of your Holy Spirit, for I have an assurance of that help in the precious promises

and sacred pledges of your loving-kindness. And again, Lord,
I thank you with all my heart. May I never forget how much I
am in your debt, but praise you all the days of my life. Amen.

Patrick's Book for Beginners

I can never thank you enough, O Father of mercies and God
of all comfort, for the benefits without number I have received
from your goodness. Knowing this I ought to take every
opportunity to bless you and to speak good of your name.
And none more so than now, for I have tasted how gracious
you are in giving your only Son, our Saviour Jesus Christ, not
only to die for me, but also to be my spiritual food and drink
in the sacrament I have received today.

When I think of what a kindness it is that I have my daily
bread and never want for the things needed in this present life,
I find I am indebted to you more than my words could ever
express.

And when I remember that you have graciously admitted
me to your own table, and fed me from it with the blessed hope
of being where my Saviour is and rejoicing with him for ever,
how far does this surpass my highest expectation? And with
what delight and satisfaction should it fill my heart?

Give to me, Lord, such a full sense of this love that I never
forget how happy I am that you have adopted us as children,
and brothers and sisters of Christ Jesus. May I always delight
in this knowledge, and fulfil the duties of a Christian life.

It is a great favour, I know, that I have the liberty to turn to
him as my most gracious Lord, and to enjoy his presence not
only in church but also at home or wherever I pray to him.

Oh, may I use these means to become more like him. May
I reflect such a strong image of him, of his goodness, humility,
patience, and meekness, that all who see me may know that I
have been with Jesus!

Let the hearts of all those who have today served, and eaten, at your holy table be glad and rejoice in you. Grant to us all, Lord, that we may leave aside the things that are contrary to our name of Christian, and go after all the things agreeable to the same. Through Christ our Lord. Amen.

Patrick's Book for Beginners

4

Taylor's Holy Living

Meditation on the Passion

All praise, honour, and glory be to the holy and eternal Jesus. I adore you, O blessed Redeemer, eternal God, the light of the Gentiles, and the glory of Israel; for you have done and suffered for me more than I could wish; more than I could think of; even all that a lost and a miserable perishing sinner could possibly need.

You were afflicted with thirst and hunger, with heat and cold, with labours and sorrows, with hard journeys and restless nights; and when you were contriving all the mysterious and admirable ways of paying our scores, you allowed yourself to be led to slaughter by those for whom in love you were ready to die.

O Lord, *what are mortals that you should consider them;
mere human beings that you should take thought for them?*

Blessed be your name, O holy Jesus; for you went about doing good, working miracles of mercy, healing the sick, comforting the distressed, instructing the ignorant, raising the dead, enlightening the blind, strengthening the lame, straightening the crooked, relieving the poor, preaching the gospel, and reconciling sinners by the mightiness of your power, by the wisdom of your Spirit, by the word of God, and the merits of your passion, your health-giving and bitter passion.

O Lord, what are mortals that you should consider them;
mere human beings that you should take thought for them?

Blessed be your name, O holy Jesus, who were content to be conspired against by your enemies, to be sold by your servant for a pitiful price, and to wash the feet of the one that took money for your life, and to give to him and to all your disciples your most holy body and blood, to become a sacrifice for their sins, even for their betraying and denying you; and for all my sins, even for my crucifying you afresh, and for many sins of which I am ashamed to think, but that the greatest of my sins magnify the infiniteness of your mercies, who did such great things for so vile a person.

O Lord, what are mortals that you should consider them;
mere human beings that you should take thought for them?

Blessed be your name, O holy Jesus, who, about to depart the world, comforted your disciples, pouring out into their ears and hearts treasures of admirable teaching; who recommended them to your Father with a mighty love, and then entered into the garden set with nothing but briars and sorrows, where you suffered a most unspeakable agony, until the sweat sighed and groaned, you fell to the ground and prayed, and what I had deserved, you suffered.

O Lord, what are mortals that you should consider them;
mere human beings that you should take thought for them?

Blessed be your name, O holy Jesus, who have sanctified to us all our natural infirmities and passions, by allowing yourself to be in fear and in trembling and amazement, by being bound and imprisoned, by being harassed and dragged with cords of violence and rough hands, by being drenched in the brook in the way, by being sought after like a thief, and used like a sinner when you are the most holy and the most innocent, cleaner than an angel and brighter than the morning star.

O Lord, what are mortals that you should consider them;
mere human beings that you should take thought for them?

Blessed be your name, O holy Jesus, and blessed be your loving-kindness and pity, by which you cared nothing for your own sorrows, and went to comfort the sadness of your disciples, enlivening their dullness, encouraging their duty, arming their weakness with excellent advice against the day of trial. Blessed be that humility and sorrow of yours, who, being Lord of the angels, yet needed and received comfort from your servant, the angel; who offered yourself to your persecutors, and made them able to seize you; and received the traitor's kiss, and permitted a veil to be thrown over your holy face, that your enemies might not come to be confounded by so bright a lustre; and would perform a miracle to cure a wound of one of the spiteful enemies; and reproved a zealous servant on behalf of a malicious adversary; and then went like a lamb to the slaughter, without noise or violence or resistance, when you could have commanded millions of angels for your guard and rescue.

O Lord, what are mortals that you should consider them;
mere human beings that you should take thought for them?

Blessed be your name, O holy Jesus, and blessed be that holy sorrow you suffered, when your disciples fled, and you were left alone in the hands of cruel men, who, like wolves in the night, thirsted for a taste of your blood; you who were led to the house of Annas, and there asked questions calculated to ensnare you, and struck on the face by him whose ear you had only just healed; and from there were dragged to the house of Caiaphas; and there all night endured the spitting, the affronts, the scorn, the blows, and all sorts of intolerable insolence; and all this for the human race, your enemy, and the cause of all your sorrows.

O Lord, what are mortals that you should consider them;
mere human beings that you should take thought for them?

Blessed be your name, O holy Jesus, and blessed be your great
mercy, who, when your servant Peter denied you and forsook
you and swore against you, not once but three times, looked
back upon him, and by that gracious and chiding look called
him back to senses and to you; who were accused before the
high-priest and railed upon, and examined to evil purposes,
all with the sole aim of your blood; who were declared guilty
of death for speaking the truth; who were sent to Pilate and
found innocent, and sent to Herod and still found innocent,
and were arrayed in white, both to declare your innocence and
yet to deride your person, and were sent back to Pilate, and
examined again, and yet nothing but innocence found in you,
and malice round about you to devour faith; and yet you still
desired more to lay down your life for them than they did to
take it from you.

O Lord, what are mortals that you should consider them;
mere human beings that you should take thought for them?

Blessed be your name, O holy Jesus, and blessed be that patience
and love, by which for our sakes you were content to be beaten
with canes, and have that holy face, which angels behold with
joy and wonder, spat upon; and be despised, when compared
with the thief Barabbas, and scourged most violently with
dirty hands until the pavement was red with that holy blood,
and condemned to a sad and shameful, a public and painful,
death, and arrayed in purple, and crowned with thorns, and
stripped naked and then clothed, and laden with the cross,
and tormented with a tablet stuck with nails at the fringes of
your garment, and bound fast with cords, and dragged most
vilely and most piteously, till the load was too great, and did
sink your tender and virginal body to the earth; and even so,

you comforted the weeping women, and had more pity for your persecutors than for yourself, and were grieved for the miseries of Jerusalem to come forty years after, more than for your present and most bitter passion.

O Lord, what are mortals that you should consider them; mere human beings that you should take thought for them?

Blessed be your name, O holy Jesus, and blessed be that incomparable sweetness and holy sorrow which you suffered, when your precious hands and feet were nailed to the cross, and the cross, being set in a hollowness of the earth, fell and tore open the wounds wider, and there, naked and bleeding, sick and faint, wounded and despised, hung upon the weight of your wounds three long hours, praying for your persecutors, satisfying your Father's wrath, reconciling the penitent thief, providing for your holy and afflicted mother, tasting vinegar and gall; and when the fullness of your suffering was accomplished, gave your soul into the hands of God, and descended to the regions of longing souls, who waited for the revelation of this your day in their prisons of hope: and then your body was transfixed with a spear, and issued forth two sacraments, water and blood, and your body was taken down for burial, and dwelt in darkness.

O Lord, what are mortals that you should consider them; mere human beings that you should take thought for them?

So, O blessed Jesus, you finished your holy passion with pain and anguish so great that nothing could be greater than it except your infinite mercy: and all this for humanity, even for me, than whom nothing could be more miserable, except you when you voluntarily became so by taking on our guilt and our punishment. And now, Lord, you who have done so much for me, be pleased only to make it effective in me, that it may not be useless and lost in me, unless I become eternally miserable, and lost to all hopes and possibility of comfort. All this deserves more love than I have to give; but, Lord, turn me all into love, and all my love into obedience, and let my obedience be without interruption, and there I hope you will accept the little I can do. Make me to be something that you delight in, and you shall have all that I am or have from you, even whatever you make fit for yourself. Teach me to live wholly for my Saviour Jesus, and to be ready to die for Jesus, and to be conformable to his life and sufferings, and to be united to him by inseparable bonds, and to have no passions but what may be servants to Jesus and disciples of his institution. O sweetest Saviour, clothe my soul with your holy robe; hide my sins in your wounds, and bury them in your grave; and let me rise in the life of grace, and abide and grow in it, until I arrive at the kingdom of glory. Amen.

Our Father . . .

Prayers of intercession

These prayers are for all types of people, and should be treated as a complete prayer, even though broken into sections.

For ourselves

O gracious Father of mercy, Father of our Lord Jesus Christ, have mercy on your servants, who bow our heads and our knees and our hearts to you; pardon and forgive us all our sins; give us the grace of holy repentance, and a strict obedience to your holy word; strengthen us in the inner person with the power of your Holy Spirit for all the parts and duties of our calling and holy living; preserve us for ever in the unity of the Holy Catholic Church, and in the integrity of the Christian faith, and in the love of God and of our neighbours, and in hope of life eternal. Amen.

For the whole Catholic Church

O holy Jesus, King of the saints, and Prince of the Catholic Church, preserve your Bride, whom you purchased with your right hand, and redeemed and cleansed with your blood, the whole Catholic Church from one end of the earth to the other; she is founded upon a rock, but planted in the sea. Preserve her safe from schism, heresy, and sacrilege. Unite all her members with the bands of faith, hope, and charity, and a visible communion. Let the daily sacrifice of prayer and sacramental thanksgiving never cease, but be for ever presented to you, and for ever prevail for the obtaining for every one of its members grace and blessing, pardon and salvation. Amen.

For all Christian rulers and governors

O King of kings and Prince of all the rulers of the earth, give your grace and Spirit to all Christian rulers and governors, the spirit of wisdom and counsel, the spirit of government and godly fear. Grant that they may live in peace and honour, that their people may love and fear them, and they may love and fear God. Speak good things into their hearts concerning the Church, that they may be nurses to her, parents to the orphans, judges and avengers of the cause of widows; that they may be compassionate to the wants of the poor, and the groans of the oppressed; that they may not vex or kill the Lord's people with unjust or ambitious wars; but may feed the flock of God, and may inquire after and do all things which promote peace, public honesty, and holy religion; so administering the things of this world that they may not fail to attain the everlasting glories of the world to come, where all your faithful people shall reign with Christ for ever. Amen.

For all that minister about holy things

O great Shepherd and Bishop of our souls, holy and eternal Jesus, give to your servants the ministers of the mysteries of Christian religion, the spirit of prudence and sanctity, faith and charity, confidence and zeal, diligence and watchfulness, that they may declare your will to your people faithfully, and dispense your sacraments rightly, and intercede with you graciously and acceptably for your servants. Grant, O Lord, that by a holy life and a true belief, by well-doing and patient suffering, they may glorify you, the great lover of souls, and, after a plentiful conversion of sinners from the errors of their ways, they may shine like the stars in glory. Amen.

Give to your servants, the bishops, a discerning spirit, that they may lay hands suddenly on no one, but may appoint such persons to the ministries of religion who may adorn the gospel of God, and whose lips may preserve knowledge, and those who by their good preaching and holy living may advance the service of the Lord Jesus. Amen.

For our nearest relatives

O God of infinite mercy, let your loving mercy and compassion descend on the head of your servants: *(name your wife, husband, children, and family)*. Be pleased to give them health of body and of spirit, sufficient in this world to comfort and support them in their journey to heaven. Preserve them from all evil and sad accidents, defend them in all assaults of their enemies, direct their souls and their actions, sanctify their hearts and words and intentions; that we all may, by the bands of obedience and charity, be united to our Lord Jesus, and, always knowing you, our merciful and gracious Father, may become a holy family discharging our whole duty in all our relations; that we in this life being your children by adoption and grace, may be admitted into your holy family in the next life, for ever to sing praises to you in the church of the first-born, in the family of your redeemed ones. Amen.

For our parents, friends and benefactors

O God, merciful and gracious, who have made my friends and my benefactors ministers of your mercy, and instruments of providence to your servant, I humbly beg a blessing to descend upon the heads of *(name the persons or the relations you wish to pray for)*. Appoint your holy angels to guard their bodies, your Holy Spirit to guide their souls, your providence to supply their needs; and let your grace and mercy preserve them from the bitter pains of eternal death, and bring them to everlasting life, through Jesus Christ. Amen.

For all in difficulty

O Lord God Almighty, you are our Father and we your children; you are our Redeemer and we your people, purchased with the price of your most precious blood; do not be angry with us lest we be consumed and brought to nothing. Let health and peace lie within our homes; let righteousness and holiness dwell for ever in our hearts, and be expressed in all our actions; and the light of your countenance be upon us in all our sufferings, that we may delight in the service and in the mercies of our God for ever. Amen.

O gracious Father and merciful God, if it is your will, say to the destroying angel, 'It is enough!', and though we are no better than those who are smitten with the rod of God, but much worse, yet may it please you, even because you are good, and because we are easily frightened and sinful and not yet fit for our appearance as creatures made in your own image, to set your mark upon our foreheads, so that your angel, the minister of your justice, may pass over us and not destroy us. Let your hand cover your servants and hide us in the clefts of the rock, in the wounds of the holy Jesus, from the present anger against us, that though we walk through the valley of the shadow of death, we may fear no evil, and suffer none; and those you have smitten with your rod support with your staff, and visit them with your mercies and salvation, through Jesus Christ. Amen.

For all pregnant women and for unborn children

O Lord God, the Father of all that trust in you, who show mercy to a thousand generations of those that fear you; have mercy on all women great with child. Be pleased to give them a joyful and a safe delivery, and let your grace preserve the fruit of their wombs, and conduct them to the holy sacrament of baptism, that they, being regenerated by your Spirit, and adopted into your family, and the portion and duty of children, may live to the glory of God, to the comfort of their parents and friends, to the edification of the Christian community, and the salvation of their own souls, through Jesus Christ. Amen.

For all men and women in the Christian Church

O holy God, eternal King, out of the infinite storehouses of your grace and mercy, give unto all virgins chastity and a religious spirit; to all persons dedicated to you and to religion, continence and meekness and active zeal and an unwearied spirit; to all married couples, faith and holiness; to widows and the fatherless, and all that are oppressed, your patronage, comfort, and defence; to all Christian women, simplicity and modesty, humility and chastity, patience and charity; give unto the poor, to all that are robbed and deprived of their goods, a competent support, and a contented spirit, and a treasure in heaven in the next life; give to prisoners and captives, to those who toil in the mines, and row in the galleys, strength of body and of spirit, liberty and redemption, comfort and restitution; to all that travel by land, your angel for their guide, and a holy and prosperous return, to all that travel by sea, freedom from pirates and shipwreck, and bring them to the haven where they wish to be; to distressed and scrupulous consciences, to melancholy and depressed persons, to all that are afflicted with evil and unclean spirits, give a light from heaven, great grace, and suitable comforts and deliverance from whatever oppresses them; give them patience and resignation; let their sorrows be changed into grace and comfort, and let the storm waft them certainly to the regions of rest and glory.

Lord God of mercy, give to your martyrs, confessors, and all your persecuted servants, constancy and prudence, boldness and hope, a full faith and a never-failing charity. To all who are condemned to death, send comfort, a strong, a quiet, and a resigned spirit; take from them the fear of death, and all remaining love of sin, and all their imperfections, and cause them to die full of grace, full of hope. And give to all the faithful, and particularly to those who have recommended themselves to the prayers of your unworthy servant, a supply of all their needs bodily and spiritual, and, according to their needs, rest and peace, pardon and refreshment, and show us all your mercy in the day of judgement. Amen.

Give, O Lord, to the magistrates and judges fairness, sincerity, courage, and prudence, that they may protect the good, defend religion, and punish the wrong-doers. Give to the nobility wisdom, valour, and loyalty; to merchants, justice and faithfulness; to all who work with their hands, truth and honesty; to our enemies, forgiveness and kindness.

Keep for us the heavens and the air in healthy state, the earth in plenty, the kingdom in peace and good government, our marriages in peace and sweetness, your people from famine and pestilence, our houses from burning and robbery, our persons from all evil, from widowhood and destitution, from violence of pains and passions, from tempests and earthquakes, from flood of waters, from rebellion or invasion, from impatience and wrong cares, from tediousness of spirit and despair, from murder, and all violent, accursed, and unusual deaths, from the surprise of sudden and violent accidents, from passionate and unreasonable fears, from all your wrath, and from all our sins. Good Lord, deliver and preserve your servants for ever. Amen.

Repress the violence of all implacable, warring, and tyrant nations; bring home into your fold all who have gone astray; call into the Church all strangers; increase the number and holiness of your own people; bring infants to ripeness of age and reason; confirm all baptized people with your grace and with your Spirit; instruct the novices and new Christians; let a great grace and merciful providence bring the young safely through the indiscretions, and passions, and temptations, of youth; and to those you have or will permit to live to a ripe old age, give competent strength and wisdom, take from them covetousness and churlishness, pride and impatience; fill them full of devotion and charity, repentance and sobriety, holy thoughts and longing desires after heaven and heavenly things; give them a holy and a blessed death, and to us all a joyful resurrection, through Jesus Christ, our Lord. Amen.

Preparation for the Holy Sacrament

An act of love

O most gracious and eternal God, the helper of the helpless, the comforter of the comfortless, the hope of the afflicted, the bread of the hungry, the drink of the thirsty, and the Saviour of all that wait on you: I bless and glorify your name, and adore your goodness, and delight in your love, that you have once more given me the opportunity of receiving the greatest favour which I can receive in this world, even the body and blood of my dearest Saviour. O take from me all love of sin or vanity; do not let my affections dwell below, but soar upwards to the element of love, to the seat of God, to the regions of glory, and the inheritance of Jesus; that I may hunger and thirst for the bread of life, and the wine of elect souls, and may know no love but the love of God, and the most merciful Jesus. Amen.

An act of desire

O blessed Jesus, you have used many ways to save me: you have given your life to redeem me, your Holy Spirit to sanctify me, yourself for my example, your word for my rule, your grace for my guide, the fruit of your body hanging on the tree of the cross for the sin of my soul; and, after all this, have sent your apostles and ministers of salvation to call me, to warn me, to return me to holiness, and peace, and happiness. Come now, Lord Jesus, come quickly: my heart desires your presence and I thirst for your grace, and would entertain you, not as a guest, but as an inhabitant, as the Lord of all my faculties. Enter in and take possession, and dwell with me for ever; that I also may dwell in the heart of my dearest Lord, which was opened for me with a spear and love.

An act of contrition

Lord, you will find my heart full of cares and worldly desires, cheated with love of riches, and neglect of holy things, proud and without restraint, false and quick to deceive itself, tied up and entangled with difficult cases of conscience, with knots which my own wildness and inconsideration and impatience have tied and shuffled together. O my dearest Lord, if you can bear to look on such an impure seat, you will see that the place to which you are invited is full of passion and prejudice, evil principles and evil habits, peevish and disobedient, lustful and intemperate, and full of sad memories, that I have often provoked you to jealousy and to anger, my dearest Saviour, who died for me, who suffered torments for me, who is infinitely good to me, and infinitely good and perfect in himself. This, O dearest Saviour, is a sad truth, and I am heartily ashamed, and truly sorrowful for it, and hate all my sins, and am full of indignation against myself for being so unworthy and careless. I humbly beg of you to increase my sorrow, and my care, and my hatred for sin; and make my love for you to swell up to a great grace, and then to glory and eternity.

An act of faith

This indeed is my sad condition; but I know, O blessed Jesus, that you took upon yourself my nature so you could suffer for my sins, and that you suffered to deliver me from them and from your Father's wrath; and I was delivered from this wrath so that I might serve you in holiness and righteousness all my days. Lord, I am as sure you did the great work of redemption for me and all humanity as I am that I am alive. This is my hope, the strength of my spirit, my joy and my confidence; never let the spirit of unbelief enter into me and take me from this rock. Here I will dwell, for I have a delight in it; here I will live, and here I desire to die.

A prayer before receiving

Therefore, O blessed Jesus, my Saviour and my God, whose body is my food, and whose righteousness is my robe, you are both priest and sacrifice, the master of the feast and the feast itself, the physician of my soul, the light of my eyes, the purifier of my stains: enter into my heart and cast out from there all impurities, all the remains of the old me; and grant that I may eat and drink of this holy sacrament with reverence, and holy enjoyment, and great effect, receiving from it the communication of your holy body and blood, for the establishment of an immovable faith, of an unfeigned love, for the fullness of wisdom, for the healing of my soul, for the blessing and preservation of my body, for the taking out of the sting of bodily death, and for the assurance of a holy resurrection; for the ejection of all evil from within me, and the fulfilling of all your righteous commandments; and to obtain for me a mercy and a fair reception at the day of judgement, through your mercies, O holy and ever-blessed Saviour Jesus.

After receiving the consecrated and blessed bread

O taste and see how gracious the Lord is: blessed is the one that trusts in him. The beasts lack and suffer hunger, but they that seek the Lord shall lack nothing that is good. Lord, what am I, that my Saviour should become my food; that the Son of God should be the meat of worms, of dust and ashes, of a sinner, of the one that was his enemy? But this you have done for me, because you are infinitely good and wonderfully gracious, and love to bless every one of us, in turning us from the evil of our ways. Enter into me, blessed Jesus: let no root of bitterness spring up in my heart, but be Lord of all my faculties. O let me feed on you by faith, and grow up by the increase of God to fullness in Christ Jesus. Amen. Lord, I believe: help my unbelief!

After receiving the cup of blessing

It is finished. Blessed be the mercies of God revealed to us in Jesus Christ. O blessed and eternal high priest, at the sacrifice of the cross, which you offered once for the sins of the whole world, and which you now and always offer in heaven to your Father by your never-ceasing intercession, and which this day has been exhibited on your holy table sacramentally, obtain mercy and peace, faith and charity, safety and establishment to your holy Church, which you have founded on a rock, the rock of a holy faith; and do not let the gates of hell prevail against her, nor the enemy of humankind take any soul out of your hand, who you have purchased with your blood, and sanctified by your Spirit. Preserve all your people from heresy and division of spirit, from scandal and the spirit of delusion, from sacrilege and hurtful persecutions.

You, O blessed Jesus, died for us: keep me for ever in holy living, from sin and sinful shame, in the communion of your Church, and your Church in safety and grace, in truth and peace, until you come again. Amen.

Dearest Jesus, since you have been pleased to enter into me, be jealous of your house and the place where your honour dwells: let no unclean spirit or unholy thought come near your dwelling lest it defile the ground where your holy feet have trodden. O teach me so to walk, that I may never bring the honour of my religion into disrepute, nor stain the holy robe which you have now put on my soul, nor break my holy promises which I have made, and you have sealed. Do not let me lose my right of inheritance, my privilege of being co-heir with Jesus, into the hope of which I have no further entered:

but be pleased to love me with the love of a father, and of a brother, and a husband, and a lord; and make me to serve you in the communion of saints, in receiving the sacrament, in the practice of all holy virtues, in the imitation of your life, and conformity to your sufferings.

May I, having now put on the Lord Jesus, desire his glory, obey his laws, and be united to his Spirit. And in the day of the Lord may I be found to have a wedding garment, and to be bearing in my body and soul the marks of the Lord Jesus, that I may enter into the joy of my Lord, and partake of his glories for ever and ever. Amen.

Conclusion

The first, and longest, section of this book is on repentance. And repentance is the key: not just to a worthy reception of the holy communion, but to everything. It is by repentance that we find forgiveness of our sins. It is by repentance that we are able to be truly *at one*, which is the meaning of atonement, the atonement Christ bought for us at the price of his body and blood: at one with our brothers and sisters and at one with Christ.

The last word, though, in this book goes not to the author but to the former Bishop of Winchester, and our father in God, Brian Duppa:

> *No human has ever invented more ways to damn themselves than God has invented ways to save us; nor has anyone ever tried more forms of sin than the Saviour has more ways to show us his mercy . . .*
>
> *The truth is, as St Bernard says, that every person who is sick with the diseases of sin has their own worst enemy within. In a vision, it was shown to him that we are the cause of our own misfortune, and though we have wounded Christ with our sin he will not leave us without remedy.*
>
> *But do not mistake what I say: I do not want you to hang your heads at this, or because the earth is not your heaven to make it your hell. For as gold keeps its name in the leaf as well as in the lump, in the coin as well as in the bullion;*

and as someone who sees a beam or two shine through the crevice of a wall may say that they see the sun just as much as someone who is out in the open; neither are we devoid of comfort.

We can say that there is a leaf of joy, a thin foil of it here, and a few glimpses of radiant sun that shine on us there. But for the full, solid, joy for which we hope, we should not look for it in this vale of tears . . . We must wait for the harvest, we must stay the course . . . until heaven is our dwelling and the angels are our partners . . . the same angels who, as Scripture says, rejoice over one repentant sinner . . .

As St Augustine says: suppose there was only one sinner in the whole world, and suppose that sinner were you. Even so, your Saviour Jesus would have come into the world. He would have suffered all that he suffered: the scorn, the violence, the passion, and that death, all for that one single soul of yours.

If God, then, would have died for a single sinner, why would the angels not be filled with joy, rejoicing for the one for whom their God would die, for you?

Of the ten lepers Christ cured, only one turned back to thank him, and there was joy in heaven for that one. Of the many sinners in Jerusalem, there was only one Mary Magdalene who washed her Saviour's feet with her tears, and there was joy in heaven for that one.

If there is only one of you who counts their conversion from this day, God the Father will bless the memory of this day for ever, for he will have gained a son or daughter; God the Son will write this day in his calendar as a red letter day, red with his own blood; God the Holy Spirit will sanctify this day for he will gain a temple in which to dwell.

And, if this is not loud enough, the angels will shout for joy, for one sinner has repented . . .

So, begin your repentance now, to complete the joy of the

angels that expect you, so that instead of your sorrows being the burden of their songs, you shall become fellow singers of their alleluias! Amen.

Sermon by Bishop Brian Duppa, preached before King Charles II

Appendix 1

Brief biographies

It is often useful to know something about the lives of people we read about. Most of these bishops have substantial biographies already, and there is only space here to give a taste of their rich and varied lives.

Archbishop William Laud

William Laud (7 October 1573 – 10 January 1645) was Archbishop of Canterbury and a fervent supporter of Charles I of England whom he encouraged to believe in the Divine Right of Kings. He was born in Reading, Berkshire, of comparatively humble origins (a fact he was to remain sensitive of through his career) and educated at Reading School and, through a White Scholarship, St John's College, Oxford.

On 5 April 1601 Laud was ordained. His Catholic tendencies and opposition to Puritanism, combined with his intellectual and organizational brilliance, soon made him a name. In those days Calvinism was on the rise in the Church of England and Laud's firm belief in the apostolic succession made him unpopular in the eyes of many.

Laud was elected President of St John's College in 1611, and made a prebendary of Lincoln Cathedral in 1614, and Archdeacon of Huntingdon the following year. He was consecrated Bishop of St David's in 1622, translated to Bath and

Wells in 1626, and made Bishop of London in 1628. Thanks to patrons, including King Charles I, he was consecrated Archbishop of Canterbury in 1633.

Laud was a firm supporter of the Church of England and a loyal Englishman. But despite this, he was continually attacked and accused of popery by the Puritans, especially his nemesis William Prynne, and his High Church stance inevitably made him unpopular and a target for ever more aggressive attacks.

A firm Archbishop, Laud believed that only total uniformity could protect the Church against those out to destroy it. An unfortunate side-effect of this firmly held, and even more firmly implemented, belief was a lack of tolerance of the views of others. In 1637, Prynne and two others had their ears removed and were branded for the crime of seditious libel.

Eventually the enemies of the Church gained the upper hand. The Long Parliament of 1640 accused Laud of treason. This resulted in his imprisonment in the Tower of London, and he was kept there during the early stages of the English Civil War.

In the spring of 1644 Laud was sent for trial, but his enemies were unable to get a conviction despite their very worst efforts. Laud's fate, though, was sealed and his martyrdom was nothing more or less than a sad inevitability.

Parliament took up the issue, and eventually decided that Laud must die. He was beheaded on 10 January 1645 on Tower Hill, even though he had been granted a royal pardon. Not that a royal pardon counted for anything in the eyes of the enemies of the Church, and, as everyone knows, Charles I was not far behind Laud in the queue for palms to celebrate their martyrdom for Christ's Church.

Bishop Lancelot Andrewes

Lancelot Andrewes (1555–1626) was born in London, of an ancient Suffolk family; his father, Thomas, was master of Trinity House. He attended the Cooper's free school, Ratcliff, in the parish of Stepney, and then the Merchant Taylors' School.

In 1571 Andrewes entered Pembroke Hall, Cambridge, proceeding MA in 1578. In 1576 he had been elected fellow of Pembroke. In 1580 he was ordained and in 1581 he was incorporated MA at Oxford.

After a period as chaplain to the Earl of Huntingdon, Andrewes became vicar of St Giles's, Cripplegate in 1588, and there delivered his striking sermons on the temptation in the wilderness and the Lord's prayer.

Andrewes was appointed prebendary of St Pancras in St Paul's, London, in 1589, and subsequently became master of his own college of Pembroke, as well as a chaplain to the Archbishop of Canterbury, John Whitgift. From 1589 to 1609 he was prebendary of Southwell.

In 1598 Andrewes declined the bishoprics of Ely and Salisbury, because of the conditions attached. In 1601 he was appointed dean of Westminster and assisted at the coronation of King James I of England. Andrewes' name is first in the list of divines appointed to make the authorized version of the Bible.

In 1605 he was consecrated Bishop of Chichester and in 1617 he accompanied James I to Scotland with a view to persuading the Scots that episcopacy was preferable to presbyterianism. In 1618 he was translated to Winchester, a diocese he administered with great success until his death in 1626.

Andrewes' position on the eucharist is more mature than that of the earlier reformers:

As to the real presence we are agreed; our controversy is as to the mode of it. As to the mode we define nothing rashly, nor anxiously investigate, any more than in the Incarnation of Christ we ask how the human is united to the divine nature in One Person. There is a real change in the elements.

Responsio, p. 263

Adoration is permitted, and the use of the terms 'sacrifice' and 'altar' maintained as being consonant with scripture and antiquity. Christ is 'a sacrifice, so to be slain; a propitiatory sacrifice, so to be eaten'.

Sermons, vol. ii, p. 296

Andrewes' best-known work is the *Manual of Private Devotions*, which has been reprinted many times, and his sermons that have been preserved are of a very high quality.

Bishop Brian Duppa

Brian Duppa (10 March 1588 – 26 March 1662), Bishop of Winchester, was born in Lewisham, Kent, son of Jeffrey Duppa, king's brewer to James I. Duppa was educated at Westminster School where Lancelot Andrewes taught him Hebrew.

He went on to Christ Church, Oxford, where he was elected fellow of All Souls in 1612, and proceeded MA in 1614. He then went travelling in France and Spain, returning to England in 1619, and proceeding BD and DD in July 1625.

He became chaplain to the Earl of Dorset, and vicar of Hailsham in 1625 and Withyham in 1627. During that time, on 23 November 1626, Duppa married his wife, Jane. They had no children.

Duppa went on to become Chancellor of Salisbury, and from there was elected Bishop of Chichester. A fairly moderate churchman, Duppa was elevated to Salisbury in December 1641.

From the execution of Charles I until the restoration of Charles II, Duppa lived quietly in Richmond, Surrey. Or, rather, appeared to live quietly: in fact he was busy writing, celebrating prayer book services, and ordaining deacons and priests. Duppa worked with others to ensure the episcopal succession survived in England, and was one of only a handful of bishops to survive the Puritan excesses. The bishops were in London in full episcopal dress to greet Charles II on his arrival on 29 May 1660.

During this time, Duppa had also taken the opportunity to revise some of his earlier devotional works, among them his incomparable *Guide to the Penitent*.

On 28 August 1660, Duppa was translated to Winchester, and within a few weeks deputized for Bishop Juxon as chief consecrator of five new bishops in Westminster Abbey. Duppa died at Richmond on 26 March 1662, knowing that he had maintained the apostolic succession in the face of a determined Puritan attempt to destroy the Church of England.

Bishop Thomas Ken

Thomas Ken (July 1637 – 19 March 1711), the most eminent of the English non-juring bishops, and one of the founding fathers of the modern English hymn, was born at Little Berkhamsted, Hertfordshire.

In 1652 Ken entered Winchester College, and in 1656 became a student of Hart Hall, Oxford. The following year, Ken moved to New College, and proceeded MA in 1664, and became a reader in logic.

Ordained at the Restoration, in 1662, Ken was given the living of Little Easton in Essex. In 1665 he resigned the living to become chaplain to Bishop Morley in Winchester. Several more livings followed, and a prebend at Winchester.

Music was always a love of Ken's life. In addition to writing hymns, he had his own organ and was a skilled lute player. There is a delightful story that he used to sing Mattins and Evensong every day, accompanying himself on the lute.

During this time, he composed two of his most famous hymns: 'Awake, my soul, and with the sun' and 'Glory to Thee, my God, this night', and worked on his *Manual of Prayers for the Use of the Scholars of Winchester College*.

In 1675 Ken set out on the Grand Tour, and in Rome he saw both the best and the worst of Roman Catholicism. This served to strengthen his regard for the Church of England, though he, like many others at this time, was often accused of popery.

In 1679, Charles II appointed Ken chaplain to the Princess Mary, the wife of William of Orange, both of whom were to play a big part in the lives of Ken and the other non-juring bishops.

In 1684, a vacancy came up in the see of Bath and Wells. Ken, now Dr Ken, was appointed bishop. He was consecrated at Lambeth on 25 January 1685, and one of his first duties was to attend the death-bed of Charles.

In 1688, when James II reissued his Declaration of Indulgence, Ken was one of the seven bishops who refused to publish it. Along with the six other bishops, Ken was committed to the Tower of London on 8 June 1688, on a charge of high misdemeanour. They were tried and acquitted.

James II soon fell, and William of Orange took the throne. Ken, having sworn allegiance to James, felt unable in good conscience to take an oath to William of Orange while James was alive. Several other bishops and priests and deacons felt the same way, and those who refused to take the oath of allegiance to William were known as the non-jurors. Most were deprived of their livings and in August 1691, Ken lost Bath and Wells.

From then on Ken lived mostly in retirement with his old school-friend Lord Weymouth at Longleat in Wiltshire. He was pressed to resume his diocese in 1703 on the death of the man who had succeeded him, but declined, partly on the ground of growing weakness, but also no doubt from his love for the quiet life of devotion to which he had become accustomed. Ken died at Longleat on 19 March 1711, a High Churchman of the old school.

Bishop Simon Patrick

Simon Patrick (8 September 1626 – 31 May 1707) was born in Gainsborough, Lincolnshire. His parents were protestants and Calvinists, and it was in this rather dour environment that the young Patrick grew up.

On 25 June 1644, Patrick was admitted to Queens' College, Cambridge, having been rejected by Emmanuel. It was at Cambridge that Patrick had the protestant, and especially the Calvinist, stuffing knocked out of him, and he proceeded MA on 18 January 1651 without a trace of the belief in the absolute predestination he once imagined had got him there.

He served his college for a number of years, becoming bursar and eventually dean. Of course, a dean must be in orders and he rather reluctantly submitted to a presbyterian 'ordination' on 8 April 1653 in London. Not believing this to be a real ordination, he sought to be ordained by a bishop with the episcopal succession, and on 5 April 1654 was ordained by Bishop Joseph Hall in a secret service at Hall's house at Potter Heigham in Norfolk.

In August 1662, the presbyterian rector of St Paul's, Covent Garden, refused to conform and was deposed. Patrick, having been treated shabbily in what should have been a certain election as President of Queens' a few years earlier, was offered this juicy living, and accepted.

In 1671, Patrick was made a royal chaplain, married in 1675, and in 1679 was made Dean of Peterborough. During this time he produced a series of excellent Old Testament commentaries and other devotional works, as well as preaching relentlessly to defend the Church of England against popery, and himself from charges of it.

In October 1689, Patrick was consecrated Bishop of Winchester. The same month, he served on the ecclesiastical commission to revise the prayer book. As he was considered an expert in the composition of prayers, he was given the job of revising the collects to bring them more into line with the epistles and gospels of the day, and many of the finest of what we often think of today as Cranmer's collects are really the work of Patrick.

In 1691 Patrick was translated to Ely. He reconstructed the bishop's palace and improved pastoral care in the diocese as well as finding the time to add to his growing collection of Old Testament commentaries. He donated a number of valuable books to the cathedral library and was a founding member of SPCK.

On 31 May 1707, Patrick died suddenly in the bishop's palace aged 80, and was buried on the north side of the presbytery, where his resting place is commemorated with a monument and epitaph erected by his successor, John Moore.

Bishop Jeremy Taylor

Jeremy Taylor (1613 – 13 August 1667) was born in Cambridge and baptized in Holy Trinity church on 15 August 1613. His father, Nathaniel, was a barber and churchwarden of Holy Trinity.

Taylor was educated at the Perse School and then Gonville and Caius College. He was ordained very young, in 1633, proceeded MA the following year, and worked as a lecturer in rhetoric at Caius.

Taylor met Archbishop William Laud when acting as a stand-in lecturer at St Paul's Cathedral for one of Laud's friends, and Laud secured for him a fellowship of All Souls, Oxford.

On 27 May 1639, Taylor married his wife, Phoebe, who was the sister of one of his pupils at Caius in 1633.

At the outbreak of the civil war, Taylor joined Charles I in Nottingham, and then Oxford, where he received his doctorate for a defence of the Church of England, *The Sacred Order and Offices of Episcopacy.*

In the meantime, he had been made rector of Uppingham in Rutland, but the parish was taken over by the parliamentary forces in May 1644. His church and rectory were plundered, his estate seized, and his wife and children thrown out. Taylor was captured and imprisoned, but soon released.

Eventually, he was allowed to retire to Wales, where he became the private chaplain of the Earl of Carbery. It was in exile in Wales that Taylor produced some of his finest work, amongst which *Holy Living* and *Holy Dying* stand out, as well as two volumes of sermons for every Sunday of the year.

His *Golden Grove* was published in 1654, and seems to have earned Taylor a spell of imprisonment, or at least house arrest, in Wales. He was imprisoned for six months during 1655, probably as a result of his outspoken rejection of the doctrine of original sin as proposed by the Puritans.

Taylor's wife, Phoebe, had died in 1651 and some time in 1655 or 1656 he married his second wife, Joanna. In the summer of 1658, the family moved to Ireland.

The ecclesiastical situation in Ireland was curious. The Church in Ireland had suffered, and most of its parishes were in the hands of presbyterians, but the persecution of Anglicans seems not to have been so severe. Even more curious was that the Irish presbyterians, unlike the Puritans in England, were royalists!

On 6 August 1660, Taylor was elected Bishop of Connor and Down, but was not consecrated until 27 January 1661, in St Patrick's Cathedral, Dublin.

Taylor and the other Irish bishops had their work cut out restoring order to the parishes. Eventually, his hard life, suffering, persecution and repeated imprisonments in England and Wales, and hard work in Ireland drove Taylor to an early grave on 13 August 1667 at the age of 54.

Bishop Thomas Wilson

Thomas Wilson (20 December 1663 – 7 March 1755) was born at Burton, Cheshire. He was taught at the home of his uncle, Richard Sherlock, who was chaplain to the Earl of Derby and Lord of Man, which accounts for Wilson's connection with the Isle.

Wilson entered Trinity College, Dublin, in 1682. He had originally wanted to study medicine, but switched to theology and was ordained to the diaconate in 1686 in the cathedral church at Kildare on the day of its consecration.

In February 1687, Wilson became curate at his uncle's parish in Winwick, near Warrington. Here he began his habit of tithing, a habit that would follow him through the rest of his life and result in him being famed for his generosity. He was ordained to the priesthood in 1689.

Wilson gave up parish work in 1692 when he was appointed domestic chaplain to Sherlock's successor as ninth Earl of Derby and Lord of Man, William Stanley.

The Church of England's smallest diocese, Sodor and Man,

became vacant in 1693. Wilson was offered the diocese but refused. After five years with no bishop, the Metropolitan Archbishop of York, in whose Province the diocese lay, became impatient with the long vacancy and complained to William III. William summoned the Earl of Derby and Lord of Man and made it known that if he did not receive a nomination in the very near future, he would fill the seat himself. Wilson was asked again, this time accepted, and was consecrated at the Savoy church in London in January 1697.

On 27 October 1698, Wilson married his wife Mary at Winwick parish church. They had one surviving son, also Thomas, and Mary died after a long illness on 7 March 1705.

Wilson's legacy to the Isle of Man is considerable. He was a very hands-on pastor and improved the efficiency of the diocese, personally organizing relief for the poor on many occasions. Roman Catholics were regular attenders at his services. Dissenters and other non-conformists were allowed to attend, and apparently even the Manx Quakers loved Wilson dearly.

In an effort to improve the literary lot of the islanders, Wilson established libraries in almost every parish, and also in Castletown and Douglas. He also made an effort to learn Manx Gaelic, eventually becoming quite proficient. In 1699 he published the first book known to be printed in Manx, the so-called *Manx Catechism*.

Probably his best-known work is *A Short and Plain Instruction for the Better Understanding of the Lord's Supper*. This excellent book was translated into Manx shortly after Wilson's death, and further translations were made into French in 1817, and Welsh in 1846.

Other devotional works and collections of sermons followed, until Wilson's death at the age of 93 on 7 March 1755, the fiftieth anniversary of his wife's death in 1705. Unlike many bishops of that time, Wilson lived on the Isle of Man all through his 58-year episcopate and records show that there was hardly an inhabitant of the island who did not turn out for the funeral procession to his final resting place in the churchyard of Kirk Michael.

Leo the Great

Leo I, or Leo the Great, was pope from 440 to 461. According to the *Liber Pontificalis* he was a native of Tuscany.

Pope Sixtus III died on 11 August 440 and Leo was unanimously elected by the people of Rome to succeed him. On 29 September he entered on a pontificate which was to be epoch-making for the centralization of the government of the Church.

Leo's sermons, of which 96 genuine examples have been preserved, are remarkable for their depth, clarity, and delightful style. The first five of these, which were delivered on the anniversaries of his consecration, show the dignity of his office, as well as his thorough conviction of the primacy of the Bishop of Rome, shown in so outspoken and decisive a manner by his whole activity as supreme pastor. Of his letters, which are of great importance for church history, 143 have come down to us: we also possess 30 letters sent to him.

Gregory the Great

Gregory I, or Gregory the Great, became pope at about the age of 50 in 590 until his death in 604. He is perhaps best known for Gregorian chant, though this was a later ascription to him, and he did not actually write any chants himself.

He is also well known as the pope who sent Augustine (not Augustine of Hippo) to Canterbury to convert the English. He saw a group of fair-haired and fair-skinned English boys in the Roman slave market one day and asked where they were from. On being told they were Angles, he joked that they were called Angles but looked like Angels, and immediately decided to secure the conversion of the English.

He is also known for his highly practical pastoral advice. Often this was given by letter, and more than 800 of his letters survive, quite a few sermons, and several longer works. Among the best of these is his *Forty Gospel Homilies*, a collection of very fine sermons.

John Chrysostom

John Chrysostom, the Golden-mouthed, was born at Antioch in Syria, around 347 and died at Commana in Pontus on 14 September 407. His surname, or nickname, 'Chrysostom' occurs for the first time in the *Constitution* of Pope Vigilius in the year 553. He is generally considered the most prominent teacher of the Greek Church and the greatest preacher ever heard in a Christian pulpit.

Chrysostom spent his early life in Antioch until, on 27 September 397, Nectarius, Bishop of Constantinople, died. There was a general rivalry in the capital, openly or in secret, for the job. After some months it was known, to the great disappointment of the competitors, that Emperor Areadius, at the suggestion of his minister Eutropius, had sent to the Prefect of Antioch to call John Chrysostom out of the town without the knowledge of the people, and to send him straight to Constantinople. In this sudden way Chrysostom was hurried to the capital, and ordained Bishop of Constantinople on 26 February 398, in the presence of a great assembly of bishops.

Constantinople was a dangerous place, full of intrigue and seething with rumours and back-stabbing. It was especially dangerous for an outspoken bishop, and Chrysostom soon upset the Empress Eudoxia with his open criticism of her and her cronies in the government.

Eudoxia allied herself with Bishop Theophilus, a deadly enemy of Chrysostom, and a series of trumped-up charges resulted in Chrysostom being sentenced to exile in June 403. But, when he had barely left the city, Eudoxia and Theophilus bowed to pressure from the people of Constantinople, and Chrysostom took his place again as bishop.

Not long after, Eudoxia had a huge silver statue of herself erected in the city. Word got back to her that Chrysostom was critical of her pompous gesture, and almost exactly a year later, on 24 June 404, Chrysostom was arrested and sent into exile again, this time never to return. He continued to exert his influence, even from exile, and an order was given in the summer of 407 to move him to the extreme limit of the empire. He fell seriously ill on the way and died on 14 September 407.

Chrysostom left behind him a huge influence and a large volume of first-class writing, both practical and theological. His sermons in particular are well-known for their quality and directness, the same directness that ultimately cost him his life.

Augustine of Hippo

Augustine (13 November 354 – 28 August 430) was born in Thagaste, in modern Tunisia, and went on to become one of the foremost African Christians of all time.

Born to a Christian mother, Monica, and a pagan father, Patrick, Augustine was brought up as a Christian. His father was converted and baptized at the end of his life. Patrick was proud of his son's achievements at school in Thagaste and Madaura and wanted to send him to Carthage to continue his education.

But the family was not rich and it took Patrick many months to save enough money to send the young Augustine. During this time Augustine gave himself up to what used to be called the 'pleasures of the flesh', and continued his downward spiral once he did get to Carthage in 370. While in Carthage, he got himself an older woman and they had a child together.

It was during this time that Augustine prayed his famous prayer: 'Lord, give me chastity. But not yet!' And these days were prominent in his later *Confessions*, in which he told the story of his life.

He also fell under the spell of the Manichees in Carthage, attracted by the simplicity of their world view: black and white, light and dark, good and evil. Eventually, after travelling to Italy and having a number of adventures there, he fell in with the brilliant bishop Ambrose of Milan and, after a few years was converted back to the Christian faith and baptized by Ambrose on Easter Day in 387. There is a story that the two of them spontaneously composed and alternately sang the verses of the *Te Deum* at Augustine's baptism. Nice story though it is, it is unlikely to be true.

Augustine made his way back to Africa and, despite his best efforts to avoid the priesthood, found a large crowd gathered around him as he prayed quietly in a church in 391. The crowd grew and began cheering and shouting for the bishop, Valerius, to ordain him.

In 396, the now elderly Valerius had Augustine consecrated assistant bishop and, after Valerius' death, Augustine continued as bishop for more than 30 years. His literary and theological output was prodigious, certainly enough to secure Augustine the place as Africa's greatest Christian thinker and writer.

In 426, at the age of 72, Augustine had his favourite deacon consecrated as his assistant. Shortly after, the Vandals invaded Africa and the elderly Augustine was caught up in the siege of

Hippo. On 28 August 430, at the ripe old age of 76, Augustine passed from death into life, leaving behind him a legacy that has shaped the Latin Churches of the West to this day.

Appendix 2

Pre-Reformation prayers

This book has concentrated on the bishops of the Church of England in the post-Reformation era, particularly the seventeenth and early eighteenth centuries. Of course, a proper understanding of the holy communion did not start then, as though it had never been heard of before. The Fathers of the Church of England simply built on the foundations of the pre-Reformation Church. Below is a small selection of prayers from the pre-Reformation Church, from the churches of both the West and the East.

The Western Churches

Preparation prayers

Most loving Lord Jesus Christ, though a sinner and trusting not in my own righteousness but in your goodness and mercy, I approach your banquet table in fear and trembling. My heart and body are defiled by many sins, and my mind and tongue I have not guarded from evil.

Therefore, O God of love and majestic awe, in the depth of my misery I fly to you, the fountain of all mercy. I run to you for healing, I hurry to your protection. And since I dare not stand before your judgement, I long to have you as my saviour.

In your sight, Lord, I lay bare my bruises and uncover my shame. I know my sins are many and grievous to you, and so I am afraid. I put my trust in your mercies, for the sum of them cannot be numbered.

So, Lord Jesus Christ, eternal King, both God and man, crucified for us, look on me with the eyes of mercy. O fountain of mercy that never runs dry, have mercy on me, who am full of sin and misery.

Hail, saving Victim, offered me and for the whole human race on the cross of shame!

Hail, noble and precious blood, flowing from the wounds of Christ to wash away the sins of the whole world!

Remember, Lord, your creature, who you have redeemed with your precious blood.

I repent of my sins. I desire to make good what I have done amiss. And so I beg you, most merciful Father, to remove far from me all my sins and failings, so that purified both in body and soul, I may worthily receive these most holy mysteries.

Grant that even as now, in my unworthiness, I intend to be a partaker of your body and blood, by that partaking I may obtain forgiveness of my sins, and be freed from my guilt.

Grant that all sinful thoughts may be banished from me, and all good intentions be born again within me, so that I may do all such good things as are pleasing to you, for protection of my body and my soul from the assaults of all my enemies. Amen.

St Ambrose of Milan

Almighty and everlasting God, look! I draw near now to the sacrament of the holy body and blood of your only-begotten Son, Jesus Christ our Lord.

I draw near, sick to the physician, filthy to the fountain of mercy, blind to the light of eternal glory, poor and needy to the Lord of heaven and earth.

And so, Lord, I beg you, from the abundance of your infinite mercy, that you would heal my sickness, wash away the filth of my sins, give light to my blind eyes, enrich my poverty and clothe my nakedness.

And then, I may receive him who is the bread of angels, the King of Kings, the Lord of Lords, with all the reverence and humility, with all the contrition and devotion, all the purity and faith, and the purpose and intention that will be profitable for the salvation of my soul.

Grant, I pray, that I may not only receive the sacrament of the body and blood of the Lord, but also the effect and operation, too.

Most gracious God, that I may so receive the body of your only-begotten Son Jesus Christ our Lord, taken by him of the Virgin Mary, that I may be incorporated into his mystical body and numbered among his friends.

Make good on your promise, most loving Father, that as I now intend in this earthly pilgrimage to receive your well-beloved Son under a veil, so I may, in the fullness of time, see him face to face; who lives and reigns with you, in the unity of the Holy Spirit, one God, now and for ever. Amen.

St Thomas Aquinas

Soul of Christ, sanctify me. Body of Christ, save me. Blood of Christ, inebriate me. Water from the side of Christ, wash me. Passion of Christ, strengthen me. O good Jesus, hear me. Within your wounds hide me. Let me not be separated from you. From the evil enemy, defend me. In the hour of my death, call me, and bid me come to you, that with all your saints I may praise you for ever and ever. Amen.

St Ignatius Loyola

Thanksgiving prayers

I give you thanks, O Lord, holy and almighty and everlasting Father, that you have enabled me, a sinner (through no merits of my own, but only by your infinite goodness and mercy) to feed on the precious body and blood of your Son, Jesus Christ our Lord.

And I pray that this holy communion may not bring on me guilt to increase my condemnation, but that it may be an effective intercession for my pardon and salvation.

Let it be to me the armour of faith, and the shield of godly resolution. Let it be profitable to me for the deliverance from all vices, for the destruction of all inclination to sin, for the increase of love and patience, of holiness and obedience, and for advancement in virtue.

Let this holy communion be my certain defence against all assaults of my enemies, both seen and unseen. Let it be effective for the subduing of all my sinful tendencies of flesh and spirit, so that I may hold fast to you, the one true God, and reach the heights of perfect happiness.

And I pray that you will allow me, a sinner, to the unspeakable joys of your heavenly banquet, where you, with your Son and the Holy Spirit, are the true light and full contentment, the everlasting joy and perfect happiness, of all your saints. Through the same Christ our Lord. Amen.

St Thomas Aquinas

Almighty and everlasting God, the saviour of souls and the redeemer of the world, look down now in your great mercy on us your servants, prostrate in spirit at the feet of your majesty.

And, in your great goodness, accept this sacrifice of praise that we have offered to you today, for the honour of your name, and for all your faithful servants, the living and the dead, and for our sins and offences.

Deliver us, we pray, from your anger. Grant us your grace and mercy. Open to us the gate of paradise. By your mighty arm, deliver us from all evils. And, whatever sins we have committed to our own condemnation, deliver us.

And grant that in this life we may persevere in your commandments, so that in the next, we may be numbered among your flock of your elect.

Grant all this to us, O God, whose name is ever blessed, and whose honour and kingdom endure to all the ages, world without end. Amen.

Western liturgies

Go before us, O Lord, in everything we do, with your most gracious favour, and maintain us with your continual help, that in everything we do, begun, continued, and ended in you, we may glorify your holy name, and finally, by your mercy, obtain everlasting life. Amen.

Western liturgies

The Eastern Churches

Preparation prayers

I know, O Lord my God, that I am not worthy that you should enter beneath the roof of the temple of my soul because it is all empty and dead, and that there is no worthy place in me for you to lay your head. But, as you were content to humble yourself by coming down from the heavens for our sake, so now you humble yourself to my humility. And as it seemed good to you to lie in a cavern and a manger of dumb beasts, so now you promise to lie in the manger of my dumb soul, and to enter my defiled body.

And, as you did not refuse to enter into the house of Simon the leper, and there to eat with sinners, so you promise to enter the house of my humble soul, leprous and sinful though it is.

And, as you did not reject the sinful woman who touched you, so also show your mercy to me, a sinner, who now come to you and touch you.

And, as you felt no loathing for the woman who kissed you, so also do not loathe my even more defiled and polluted lips and my unclean tongue.

But may the fiery coal of your pure body and of your precious blood be for me sanctification, enlightenment, and health for my humble soul and body. May they be for me the lightening of the burden of my many sins, preservation from the workings of the devil, cleansing of my wicked way of life, mortification of passions, instruction in your commandments, the acquiring of divine grace, and the inheritance of your kingdom.

For I come to you, O Christ-God, not with contempt, but trusting in your unspeakable goodness, and so that my absenting myself from communion with you may not result in me being seized by the hungry but invisible wolf.

So, I pray, O holy master, sanctify my soul and body, my mind and heart, all my inner being, and make me a new creation. Establish me in the fear of you, and make my sanctification complete and eternal.

Be my helper and defender, guiding my life in peace, and enabling me to stand at your right hand with your Mother, all your holy ones, the angels and the heavenly hosts, and all the saints who, through all the ages, have been well-pleasing to you. Amen.

Ascribed to St John Chrysostom

I stand before the doors of your temple, yet I do not refrain from wicked thoughts. But, O Christ-God, who justified the publican, who showed mercy to the woman of Canaa, and opened the doors of paradise to the repentant thief: open also to me your loving-kindness and accept me who am here and who touch you, as you accepted the sinful woman and the woman with an issue of blood. One of them through touching the hem of your garment, received perfect healing; the other, clasping your pure feet, went away with her sins forgiven. And do not let me be consumed, even though I am cursed by my sins, through daring to receive your body. But accept me as you accepted them; illumine my spiritual senses, and consume my sinful offences. For you are blessed, to the ages of ages. Amen.

Ascribed to St John of Damascus

I believe and I confess, O Lord, that you are indeed the Truth, the Christ, the Son of the living God, who came into the world to save sinners, of who I am foremost. And I believe that his is indeed your pure body and your precious blood. And so, I beg you, have mercy on me, and forgive my sins both voluntary and involuntary, of word and deed, committed with knowledge or in ignorance. And promise me that I may partake without con-demnation of your pure mysteries, to the forgiveness of sins, and to eternal life. Amen.

Ascribed to St John Chrysostom

Thanksgiving prayers

We give you thanks, O Lord, the lover of the human race and benefactor of our souls and bodies, that you have fed us today with your heavenly and immortal mysteries. Guide our path, establish us in fear of you, and guard our life, make certain our steps, through the prayers and intercession of the glorious birth-giver of God and ever-Virgin Mary, and of all the saints. Amen.

Liturgy named in honour of St John Chrysostom

We give you thanks, O Lord our God, for the participation in your holy, pure, immortal and heavenly mysteries, which you have given us today for the safe-keeping and sanctification and healing of our souls and bodies. And you, Lord of all, grant that the communion of the holy body and blood of your Christ may be for us a faith without confusion, a love that cannot fail, an increase of wisdom, healing of body and soul, the repelling of every enemy, the fulfilment of your commandments, and an acceptable defence at the judgement seat of your Christ. Amen.

Liturgy named in honour of St Basil the Great

Let our mouths be filled with your praise, O Lord, that we may tell of your glory, for you have permitted us to be partakers of your holy, divine, and life-giving mysteries. Make us certain in our sanctification, that we may meditate on your righteousness all the day long!

Eastern liturgies

May your holy body, O Lord Jesus Christ our God, profit me to life eternal, and your precious blood to the forgiveness of my sins. May this eucharist be for me joy and health and gladness, and enable me, a sinner, to stand worthily at the right hand of your glory in your terrible and second coming; through the intercessions of your pure Mother, and of all your saints. Amen.

Eastern liturgies

Appendix 3

Scriptural imagery in prayer

Many of the prayers, litanies and meditations collected in this book echo Scripture, often the Old Testament. Sometimes this scriptural imagery is obvious, at other times less so and may just feel familiar as you pray without you being able to put your finger on what it is.

The Psalms are a common source of imagery in Christian prayer. The Psalter is even sometimes called the Church's hymnbook, and has been a rich source of inspiration for many Christians down the centuries. But, even in this short collection, the imagery, the pictures painted in words by the bishops, come from many parts of scripture, both old and new.

The prayers in this collection have deliberately not been footnoted or referenced in any way, so as not to disturb the flow of prayer: it is very tempting to see a reference and feel an uncontrollable urge to follow it, rather than continuing to read or pray.

The following up of references is left as what used to be called 'an exercise for the reader' in the days before even devotional books became cluttered with references and footnotes. But, to help the reader along, and give a few hints, here is just one paragraph of one of Archbishop William Laud's prayers again, this time referenced. These references could be seen as 'further reading', for instance. They are not intended to be exhaustive references, just what occurred to the author as he was writing this appendix: you will certainly find others, even in this one short prayer.

The references use the NRSV verse-numbering scheme: if you use a different version, your mileage may vary.

O Lord, I have fallen short in many things,[1] *I have acted wrongly,*[2] *and caused sadness to your most Holy Spirit,*[3] *I have provoked the compassion of your kindness*[4] *by thought,*[5] *word*[6] *and deed,*[7] *by night and by day,*[8] *openly and in secret,*[9] *intentionally and unintentionally.*[10] *If you were to show me my sins,*[11] *if you were to require an account from me for those sins known to you that I have committed knowingly,*[12] *what should I do? Where should I hide?*[13] *But in your anger Lord, do not accuse me, nor reproach me in your wrath.*[14] *Rather, pity me,*[15] *not only because I am weak and sick,*[16] *but because I am the work of your own hand.*[17] *I beg you, do not enter into judgement with your servant,*[18]

---

1 Romans 3.23
2 Daniel 9.5; Baruch 2.12
3 Isaiah 63.10; Matthew 12.32; Acts 7.51; Ephesians 4.30
4 Psalm 78.41, 78.58; Jeremiah 7.19; Manasseh 1.10
5 James 2.4
6 Matthew 12.36
7 Ezra 9.13; Ecclesiastes 8.11; Zechariah 1.4; 2 Esdras 1.5; Colossians 1.21
8 Nehemiah 1.6
9 Psalm 90.8; Wisdom 17.3
10 See the books of Leviticus, Numbers and Deuteronomy for the distinction between intentional and unintentional sins, and Hebrews 9.7
11 Job 13.23
12 Matthew 12.36; Luke 16
13 Psalm 139:3–end
14 Psalm 27.9, and also Isaiah 12.1
15 Psalm 86.16
16 Psalm 6.1–4
17 Job 10.3; 14.15; Ephesians 2.10
18 Psalm 143.2

for if you, O Lord, should mark iniquities, Lord, who could stand?[19] *Surely not I, if anyone at all.*[20] *For I am adrift in a sea of sin, and am not worthy to be received into heaven on account of the multitude of my sins,*[21] *which are without number,*[22] *my shameful deeds, injustices and the rest,*[23] *and a thousand more of the unspeakable passions from which I have not left off.*[24]

The other prayers are all full of scriptural imagery in much the same way. The seventeenth-century divines knew their scripture, often almost by heart, and it pervades their thought, their teaching, their preaching, and their praying. This depth of knowledge of the scriptures is not unlike that of the early Church Fathers, and a welcome change from the rather dry and rigid scholasticism of the Western Church in the preceding centuries.

Unfortunately, it is not possible to do this for every prayer in this collection: the footnotes would be at least three times longer than the text, and there is a very real danger that the book would cease to be a collection designed to be used and become a dry and rather academic work.

Instead, pray the prayers: repent of your sins, discern the body, and return your thanks to the Lord!

---

19 Psalm 130.3

20 Psalm 76.7; Nahum 1.2–6; Malachi 3.1, 2; Luke 21.36; Revelation 6.15–17

21 See the story of the prodigal son in Luke 15, a very common motif in penitential prayer

22 Psalm 40.12

23 Ezekiel 7.10

24 Romans 6.12

Appendix 4

Texts used for this book

A very large number of books were read in researching this book. Quite a few of these books were subsequently used in preparing it, and a very short introduction to each book is included in this appendix. Throughout the text of the main part of this book, a very short note appears after each prayer with the name of the author or compiler and an abbreviated title. These notes act as a key to this appendix, where more details of each book used are given.

Laud's Private Devotions

This selection of prayers is from Archbishop William Laud's *Private Devotions*. The edition used for this selection is *A Summarie of Devotions Compiled and Used by Dr William Laud, Sometime Ld Arch-bishop of Canterbvry : now Published according to the Copy Written with his Own Hand and Reserved in the Archives of St. John Baptist's Colledge Library in Oxon*, published in Oxford in 1667, more than twenty years after Laud's martyrdom, and which, as the title says, was transcribed from Laud's hand-written notebooks containing the devotions.

Andrewes' Private Devotions

Bishop Lancelot Andrewes' *Manual of Private Devotions* is a masterful compilation of notes, prayers and helps. Some of it is in English, but a lot of it is in Greek and Latin. The prayers in this section are from the Greek part of the devotions. They are mostly extracts from the liturgies of Eastern Orthodox churches.

Duppa's Guide for the Penitent

One of the finest works on repentance ever published was Bishop Brian Duppa's *A Guide for the Penitent, or, a Model Drawn up for the Help of a Devout Soul Wounded with Sin*, first published in London in 1664. This marvellous book contains a great deal of advice on repentance and reception of the holy communion, and three parts of it are used in this collection: a selection of prayers from the first part of the book preparing for the devotions, and the incomparable 'Litany of confession' and 'Penitent's prayer'. The author hopes one day, and God willing, to produce a complete modern-English edition of this work. The first edition was used for this selection.

Duppa's Holy Rules and Helps

Some of the prayers are taken from the second part of another of Bishop Brian Duppa's excellent books, *Holy Rules and Helps to Devotion, both in Prayer and Practice*, published in London in 1673. The first edition was used for this selection.

Ken's Manual of Prayers

Shortly after the Restoration, in the second half of the seventeenth century, Thomas Ken produced a book of devotions for the students at Winchester College, where he had been a student and then a fellow himself. This book, the *Manual of Prayers for the Use of the Scholars of Winchester College*, though designed for students, is a superb resource, and the 1675 edition, printed in London, was used for this selection from Bishop Ken.

Patrick's Book for Beginners

This little-known Bishop of Ely, who deserves far greater recognition than he has had, wrote a very nice work called *A Book for Beginners, or, A help to Young Communicants that may be Fitted for the Holy Communion, and Receive it with Profit*. The second edition, printed in London in 1680, was used for this collection.

Taylor's Holy Living

In his book *Holy Living*, Bishop Jeremy Taylor provides a complete system of preparation for receiving the holy communion. The edition used for this collection is the author's own copy of *Holy Living* published in 1905 by SPCK, which was carefully checked against the relevant section of *Holy Living : in which are Described the Means and Instruments of Obtaining Every Virtue, and the Remedies against Every Vice, and Considerations Serving to the Resisting all Temptations : together with Prayers Containing the Whole Duty of a Christian, and the Parts of Devotion Occasians* [sic], *and Furnished for All*

Necessities, the fifth edition of the work, with corrections to earlier editions and some additions, published in London in 1656. Where there are differences, the 1656 edition was used for this collection.

Wilson's Lord's Supper

Bishop Thomas Wilson's *A Short and Plain Instruction for the Better Understanding of the Lord's Supper*, first published in English in 1734 and soon translated into Manx, the language of the Isle of Man, for the benefit of parishioners on the island, is used for this selection. The edition used for this collection was volume four of *The Works of the Right Reverend Father in God, Thomas Wilson, D.D., Lord Bishop of Sodor and Man* in the Library of Anglo-Catholic Theology, Oxford, 1851.

Anonymous Guide to Young Communicants

Several prayers are from the fourth edition of a marvellous little book, published anonymously in London in 1695: *A Guide to Young Communicants: or, The Whole Duty of the Sacrament Fitted for Those that Desire to be Worthy Receivers of the Lords Supper: with Suitable Prayers, for Morning and Evening. Also Directions for a Holy Living and Dying. A Dialogue between a Divine and a Beggar. And a Description of Christ's Person when on Earth. To which is added, Bishop Usher's Prophecy.* Unfortunately, nothing is known of the author.